The Reconstruction and Development Programme

The Reconstruction and Development Programme

A policy framework

African National Congress
1994

First published in 1994 for
African National Congress (ANC)
Johannesburg, South Africa

by Umanyano Publications
P.O. Box 3851
Johannesburg 2000

ISBN 0-9583834-1-3

Cover design by Manik Designs
Photographs by the Photographic Unit of the ANC Department of
Information and Publicity
Text design and layout by Annette Griessel
Printed by ABC Printers & Book Printers, Cape Town

Preface

This document – The Reconstruction and Development Programme (RDP) – is the end of one process and the beginning of another. The document is the result of many months of consultation within the ANC, its Alliance partners and other mass organisations in the wider civil society. This consultation has resulted in the policy framework contained in this document.

The process now underway is that of developing the detailed policy and legislative programme necessary to implement the RDP. In preparing the document, and in taking it forward, we are building on the tradition of the Freedom Charter. In 1955, we actively involved people and their organisations in articulating their needs and aspirations. Once again we have consulted widely.

However, in 1994 we are about to assume the responsibilities of government and must go beyond the Charter to an actual programme of government. This RDP document is a vital step in that process. It represents a framework that is coherent, viable and has widespread support. The RDP was not drawn up by experts – although many, many experts have participated in that process – but by the very people that will be part of its implementation. It is a product of consultation, debate and reflection on what we need and what is possible. For those who have participated in the process it has been invigorating and reaffirmed the belief that the people of our country are indeed its greatest asset.

The RDP has gone through six drafts. This document incorporates the numerous comments and proposals arising from our Conference on Reconstruction and Strategy in January. In the process there has been much public comment – both favourable and critical. We welcome this, even though we may not always agree with the comment. However, in many cases, both public and private comments have made very valuable contributions and caused us to rethink because by doing so the greater interests of all will be served.

With this document we will now consult very widely to ensure that all considered views are available to the policy making process. We are encouraging local communities to begin developing their own priorities. Within this framework we are able to organise and develop further the vast amount of research and information available to us in the developing of detailed policy.

The ANC and its Alliance partners have principles and policies to which we are deeply committed, but we will not close our ears to other viewpoints. Let me encourage all to express those viewpoints. Democracy will have little content, and indeed, will be short lived if we cannot address our socio-economic problems within an expanding and growing economy. The ANC is committed to carrying out these programmes with the support of its allies and our people.

From 26–28 April each of us has a right to exercise a choice – without doubt one of the most important choices any of us will ever make. That choice will determine our socio-economic future and that of our children. Join us in the patriotic endeavour to ensure that all our people share in that future.

Nelson Rolihlahla Mandela
1994

Contents

1.
Introduction to the Reconstruction and Development Programme

1.1 WHAT IS THE RECONSTRUCTION AND DEVELOPMENT PROGRAMME (RDP)?

1.1.1.   The RDP is an integrated, coherent socio-economic policy framework. It seeks to mobilise all our people and our country's resources toward the final eradication of apartheid and the building of a democratic, non-racial and non-sexist future.

1.1.2.   Within the framework for policy represented by the RDP, the ANC will develop detailed positions and a legislative programme of government.

1.1.3.   The RDP has been drawn up by the ANC-led alliance in consultation with other key mass organisations. A wide range of non-governmental organisations (NGOs) and research organisations assisted in the process.

1.1.4.   This process of consultation and joint policy formulation must continue as the RDP is developed into an effective programme of government. Other key sectors of our society such as the business community must be consulted and encouraged to participate as fully as they may choose.

1.1.5.   Those organisations within civil society that participated in the development of the RDP will be encouraged by an ANC government to be active in and responsible for the effective implementation of the RDP.

1.1.6. This inclusive approach to developing and implementing policy is unique in South Africa's political history. The special nature of the ANC as a liberation movement and the traditions of the Freedom Charter make it the only political organisation capable of unifying a wide range of social movements, community-based organisations and numerous other sectors and formations. Widespread and broad-based extra-parliamentary support will allow the ANC within a Government of National Unity to implement the programme.

1.2 WHY DO WE NEED AN RDP?

1.2.1. Our history has been a bitter one dominated by colonialism, racism, apartheid, sexism and repressive labour policies. The result is that poverty and degradation exist side by side with modern cities and a developed mining, industrial and commercial infrastructure. Our income distribution is racially distorted and ranks as one of the most unequal in the world – lavish wealth and abject poverty characterise our society.

1.2.2. The economy was built on systematically enforced racial division in every sphere of our society. Rural areas have been divided into underdeveloped bantustans and well-developed, white-owned commercial farming areas. Towns and cities have been divided into townships without basic infrastructure for blacks and well-resourced suburbs for whites.

1.2.3. Segregation in education, health, welfare, transport and employment left deep scars of inequality and economic inefficiency. In commerce and industry, very large conglomerates dominated by whites control large parts of the economy. Cheap labour policies and employment segregation concentrated skills in white hands. Our workers are poorly equipped for the rapid changes taking place in the world economy. Small and medium-sized enterprises are underdeveloped, while highly protected industries underinvested in research, development and training.

1.2.4. The result is that in every sphere of our society – economic, social, political, moral, cultural, environmental – South Africans are confronted by serious problems. There is not a single sector of South African society, nor a person living in South Africa, untouched by the ravages of apartheid. Whole regions of our country are now suffering as a direct result of the apartheid policies and their collapse.

1.2.5.   In its dying years, apartheid unleashed a vicious wave of violence. Thousands and thousands of people have been brutally killed, maimed, and forced from their homes. Security forces have all too often failed to act to protect people, and have frequently been accused of being implicated in, and even fermenting, this violence. We are close to creating a culture of violence in which no person can feel any sense of security in their person and property. The spectre of poverty and/or violence haunts millions of our people.

1.2.6.   Millions of ordinary South Africans struggled against this system over decades, to improve their lives, to restore peace, and to bring about a more just society. In their homes, in their places of work, in townships, in classrooms, in clinics and hospitals, on the land, in cultural expression, the people of our country, black, white, women, men, old and young devoted their lives to the cause of a more humane South Africa. This struggle against apartheid was fought by individuals, by political organisations and by a mass democratic movement.

1.2.7.   It is this collective heritage of struggle, these common yearnings, which are our greatest strength, and the RDP builds on it. At the same time the challenges facing South Africa are enormous. Only a comprehensive approach to harnessing the resources of our country can reverse the crisis created by apartheid. Only an all-round effort to harness the life experience, skills, energies and aspirations of the people can lay the basis for a new South Africa.

1.2.8.   The first decisive step in this direction will be the forthcoming one-person, one-vote elections. A victory for democratic forces in these elections will lay the basis for effective reconstruction and development, and the restoration of peace.

1.2.9.   But an election victory is only a first step. No political democracy can survive and flourish if the mass of our people remain in poverty, without land, without tangible prospects for a better life. Attacking poverty and deprivation must therefore be the first priority of a democratic government.

1.2.10.   How can we do this successfully? It is no use merely making a long list of promises that pretend to answer every need expressed. Making promises is easy – especially during election campaigns – but carrying them out as a government is very much more difficult. A programme is required that is achievable, sustainable, and meets the objectives of freedom and an improved standard of living and quality of life for all South Africans within a peaceful and stable society.

1.2.11.   The RDP is designed to be such a programme. To reach the RDP's objectives we face many obstacles and we are setting ourselves a great challenge. Each and every expectation will not be realised and each and every need will not be met immediately. Hard choices will have to be made. The RDP provides the framework within which those choices can be made. Even more importantly, it will involve both government and the people in further identifying needs and the obstacles to satisfying those needs, and will involve both in jointly implementing realistic strategies to overcome these obstacles. The RDP is an expression of confidence in the wisdom, organisational abilities and determination of our people.

1.3   THE SIX BASIC PRINCIPLES OF THE RDP

1.3.1.   Six basic principles, linked together, make up the political and economic philosophy that underlies the whole RDP. This is an innovative and bold philosophy based on a few simple but powerful ideas. They are:

1.3.2.   **An integrated and sustainable programme.** The legacy of apartheid cannot be overcome with piecemeal and uncoordinated policies. The RDP brings together strategies to harness all our resources in a coherent and purposeful effort that can be sustained into the future. These strategies will be implemented at national, provincial and local levels by government, parastatals and organisations within civil society working within the framework of the RDP.

This programme is essentially centred on:

1.3.3.   **A people-driven process.** Our people, with their aspirations and collective determination, are our most important resource. The RDP is focused on our people's most immediate needs, and it relies, in turn, on their energies to drive the process of meeting these needs. Regardless of race or sex, or whether they are rural or urban, rich or poor, the people of South Africa must together shape their own future. Development is not about the delivery of goods to a passive citizenry. It is about active involvement and growing empowerment. In taking this approach we are building on the many forums, peace structures and negotiations that our people are involved in throughout the land.

This programme and this people-driven process are closely bound up with:

1.3.4.   **Peace and security for all.** Promoting peace and security must involve all people and must build on and expand the National Peace Initiative. Apartheid placed the security forces, police and judicial system at the service of its racist ideology. The security forces have been unable to stem the tide of violence that has engulfed our people. To begin the process of reconstruction and development we must now establish security forces that reflect the national and gender character of our country. Such forces must be non-partisan, professional, and uphold the Constitution and respect human rights. The judicial system must reflect society's racial and gender composition, and provide fairness and equality for all before the law.

As peace and security are established, we will be able to embark upon:

1.3.5.   **Nation-building.** Central to the crisis in our country are the massive divisions and inequalities left behind by apartheid. We must not perpetuate the separation of our society into a 'first world' and a 'third world' – another disguised way of preserving apartheid. We must not confine growth strategies to the former, while doing patchwork and piecemeal development in the latter, waiting for trickle-down development. Nation-building is the basis on which to build a South Africa that can support the development of our Southern African region. Nation-building is also the basis on which to ensure that our country takes up an effective role within the world community. Only a programme that develops economic, political and social viability can ensure our national sovereignty.

Nation-building requires us to:

1.3.6.   **Link reconstruction and development.** The RDP is based on reconstruction and development being parts of an integrated process. This is in contrast to a commonly held view that growth and development, or growth and redistribution are processes that contradict each other. Growth – the measurable increase in the output of the modern industrial economy – is commonly seen as the priority that must precede development. Development is portrayed as a marginal effort of redistribution to areas of urban and rural poverty. In this view, development is a deduction from growth. The RDP breaks decisively with this approach. If growth is defined as an increase in output, then it is of course a basic goal. However, where that growth occurs, how sustainable it is, how it is distributed, the degree to which it contributes to building long-term productive capacity and human resource development, and what impact it has on the environment, are the crucial questions when considering reconstruction and development. The RDP integrates growth, development, reconstruction and redistribution into a unified programme. The key to this link is an infrastructural programme that will provide access to modern and effective services like electricity, water, telecommunications, transport, health, education and training for all our people. This programme will both meet basic needs and open up previously suppressed economic and human potential in urban and rural areas. In turn this will lead to an increased output in all sectors of the economy, and by modernising our infrastructure and human resource development, we will also enhance export capacity. Success in linking reconstruction and development is essential if we are to achieve peace and security for all.

Finally, these first five principles all depend on a thoroughgoing

1.3.7. **Democratisation of South Africa.** Minority control and privilege in every aspect of our society are the main obstruction to developing an integrated programme that unleashes all the resources of our country. Thoroughgoing democratisation of our society is, in other words, absolutely integral to the whole RDP. The RDP requires fundamental changes in the way that policy is made and programmes are implemented. Above all, the people affected must participate in decision-making. Democratisation must begin to transform both the state and civil society. Democracy is not confined to periodic elections. It is, rather, an active process enabling everyone to contribute to reconstruction and development.

1.3.8. An **integrated programme**, based on the **people**, that **provides peace and security for all** and **builds the nation**, **links reconstruction and development** and deepens **democracy** – these are the six basic principles of the RDP.

1.4 THE KEY PROGRAMMES OF THE RDP

1.4.1. There are many proposals, strategies and policy programmes contained in the RDP. These can be grouped into five major policy programmes that are linked one to the other. The five key programmes are:

- meeting basic needs;
- developing our human resources;
- building the economy;
- democratising the state and society, and
- implementing the RDP.

1.4.2. **Meeting Basic Needs.** The first priority is to begin to meet the basic needs of people – jobs, land, housing, water, electricity, telecommunications, transport, a clean and healthy environment, nutrition, health care and social welfare. In this way we can begin to reconstruct family and community life in our society. In this chapter, achievable programmes are set out for the next five years. These include programmes to redistribute a substantial amount of land to landless people, build over one million houses, provide clean water and sanitation to all, electrify 2,5 million new homes and provide access for all to affordable health care and telecommunications. The success of these programmes is essential if we are to achieve peace and security for all.

1.4.3. Our people should be involved in these programmes by being made part of the decision-making on where infrastructure is located, by being employed in its construction and by being empowered to manage and administer these large-scale programmes. These major infrastructural programmes should stimulate the economy through increased demand for materials such as bricks and steel, appliances such as television sets and washing machines, and many other products. In addition, the industrial sector must develop new, more efficient and cheaper products to meet our basic infrastructural needs.

1.4.4. **Developing Our Human Resources.** The RDP is a people-centred programme – our people must be involved in the decision-making process, in implementation, in new job opportunities requiring new skills, and in managing and governing our society. This will empower our people but an education and training programme is crucial. This chapter of the RDP deals with education from primary to tertiary level, from child care to advanced scientific and technological training. It focuses on young children, students and adults. It deals with training in formal institutions and at the workplace.

1.4.5. The underlying approach of these programmes is that education and training should be available to all from cradle to grave. The RDP takes a broad view of education and training, seeing it not only as something that happens in schools or colleges, but in all areas of our society – homes, workplaces, public works programmes, youth programmes and in rural areas.

1.4.6.   A key focus throughout the RDP is on ensuring a full and equal role for women in every aspect of our economy and society. With this emphasis and with the emphasis on affirmative action throughout the RDP, we must unlock boundless energies and creativity suppressed by racism and discrimination.

1.4.7.   In training, particular attention is paid to the challenges posed by the restructuring of our industries as we fully re-enter the world economy. These challenges can only be met through the extensive development of our human resources.

1.4.8.   An arts and culture programme is set out as a crucial component of developing our human resources. This will assist us in unlocking the creativity of our people, allowing for cultural diversity within the project of developing a unifying national culture, rediscovering our historical heritage and assuring that adequate resources are allocated.

1.4.9.   Because of apartheid, sport and recreation have been denied to the majority of our people. Yet there can be no real socio-economic development without there being adequate facilities for sport and recreation in all communities. The RDP wants to ensure that all people have access to such facilities. Only in this way can all our peoples have a chance to represent their villages, towns, cities, provinces or country in the arena of sport and to enjoy a rich diversity of recreational activities.

1.4.10.   The problems facing the youth are well known. If we are to develop our human resource potential, then special attention must be paid to the youth. Our human resource policy should be aimed at reversing youth marginalisation, empowering youth, and allowing them to reach their full potential. Programmes for training, education and job creation will enable our youth to play a full role in the reconstruction and development of our society.

1.4.11.   This programme for the development of our human resources underpins the capacity to democratise our society, thus allowing people to participate on the basis of knowledge, skill and creativity.

1.4.12. **Building the Economy.** The economy has strengths and weaknesses. Mining, manufacturing, agriculture, commerce, financial services and infrastructure are well developed. At present we have a large surplus of electricity. These are strengths we can build on. But so far they have not benefitted all our people. A process of reconstruction is proposed to ensure that these strengths now benefit all our people.

1.4.13. But we must also address serious weaknesses in our economy. There are still very clear racial and gender inequalities in ownership, employment and skills. Past industrial policies assisted in creating employment and were an important factor in developing industry but they were also accompanied by repressive labour practices, neglect of training, isolation from the world economy and excessive concentration of economic power. The result is a low level of investment in research and development, low and inappropriate skill levels, high costs, low productivity and declining employment.

1.4.14. Central to building the economy is the question of worker rights. Past policies of labour exploitation and repression must be redressed and the imbalances of power between employers and workers corrected. The basic rights to organise and to strike must be entrenched. And negotiations and participative structures at national, industry and workplace level must be created to ensure that labour plays an effective role in the reconstruction and development of our country.

1.4.15. In the world economy, the demand for raw materials including minerals has not grown rapidly and there is intense competition in the production of manufactured goods. The General Agreement on Trade and Tariffs (GATT) was recently updated to achieve substantial reductions in tariff levels. Our economy must adjust to these pressures if we are to sustain economic growth and continue to develop a large domestic manufacturing sector that makes greater use of our own raw materials and minerals.

1.4.16. A central proposal in this chapter is that we cannot build the South African economy in isolation from its

Southern African neighbours. Such a path would benefit nobody in the long run. If South Africa attempts to dominate its neighbours it will restrict their growth, reducing their potential as markets, worsening their unemployment, and causing increased migration to South Africa. If we seek mutual cooperation, we can develop a large stable market offering stable employment and common labour standards in all areas.

1.4.17. The pressures of the world economy and the operations of international organisations such as the International Monetary Fund (IMF), World Bank and GATT, affect our neighbours and South Africa in different ways. In the case of our neighbours, they were pressured into implementing programmes with adverse effects on employment and standards of living. It is essential that we combine to develop effective strategies for all Southern African countries.

1.4.18. In building the economy, programmes dealing with the following areas are dealt with: linking reconstruction and development; industry, trade and commerce; resource-based industries; upgrading infrastructure; labour and worker rights, and Southern Africa.

1.4.19. **Democratising the State and Society.** Democratisation is integral to the RDP. Without thoroughgoing democratisation the resources and potential of our country and people will not be available for a coherent programme of reconstruction and development.

1.4.20. In linking democracy, development and a people-centred approach, we are paving the way for a new democratic order. This chapter sets out the role of the Constitution and Bill of Rights, of national, provincial and local government, the administration of justice, the public sector, parastatals, the police and security forces, social movements and NGOs, and a democratic information system in facilitating socio-economic development.

1.4.21. **Implementing the RDP.** The RDP raises many challenges in its implementation because it involves processes and forms of participation by organisations outside government that are very different to the old apartheid order. To implement and coordinate the RDP will require the establishment of effective RDP structures in government at a national, provincial and local level.

1.4.22. This chapter deals with the proposals for coordinating and planning the implementation of the RDP. This requires substantial restructuring of present planning processes and a rationalisation of the complex, racist and fragmented structures that exist. The RDP can only be people-centred if the planning and coordinating processes allow the active involvement of democratic structures.

1.4.23. Understandably, the first questions asked are: What will the RDP cost? Who will pay for it? These are important questions and in developing a programme to finance the RDP, certain key points are taken into account:

1.4.23.1. most of the expenditure on the RDP is not in fact new – rather it is the better organisation and rationalisation of existing systems that will unlock resources;

1.4.23.2. we must improve the capacity of the financial sector to mobilise more resources and to direct these to activities set out in the RDP, from housing to small and medium-sized enterprises;

1.4.23.3. we must ensure that electrification and telecommunications will be self-financing;

1.4.23.4. existing funds must be reallocated and rationalisation must be effected in many areas;

1.4.23.5. improved and reformed tax systems will collect more tax without having to raise tax levels (as the RDP succeeds, more taxpayers will be able to pay and revenue will rise), and

1.4.23.6. new funds will be raised in a number of areas.

1.5   CONCLUSION

1.5.1.   All over South Africa, including in People's Forums, the same questions are posed over and over:

- how will the ANC create jobs?
- when will you build houses?
- how can we get water and electricity?
- what about education?
- when will we have a fair and effective police force?
- will you give us health care?
- what about pensions?

1.5.2.   The RDP attempts to provide achievable, realistic and clear programmes to answer these questions. But it goes further than this and encourages people and their organisations to participate in the process. In the conclusion we outline proposed concrete steps to make such participation possible.

2.
Meeting Basic Needs

2.1 PROBLEM STATEMENT

2.1.1.   Poverty is the single greatest burden of South Africa's people, and is the direct result of the apartheid system and the grossly skewed nature of business and industrial development which accompanied it. Poverty affects millions of people, the majority of whom live in the rural areas and are women. It is estimated that there are at least 17 million people surviving below the Minimum Living Level in South Africa, and of these at least 11 million live in rural areas. For those intent on fermenting violence, these conditions provide fertile ground.

2.1.2.   It is not merely the lack of income which determines poverty. An enormous proportion of very basic needs are presently unmet. In attacking poverty and deprivation, the RDP aims to set South Africa firmly on the road to eliminating hunger, providing land and housing to all our people, providing access to safe water and sanitation for all, ensuring the availability of affordable and sustainable energy sources, eliminating illiteracy, raising the quality of education and training for children and adults, protecting the environment, and improving our health services and making them accessible to all.

2.1.3.   With a per capita gross national product (GNP) of more than R8 500 South Africa is classified as an upper middle income country. Given its resources, South Africa can afford to feed, house, educate and provide health care for all its citizens. Yet apartheid and economic exploitation have created the gross and unnecessary inequalities among us. Unlocking existing resources for reconstruction and development will be a critical challenge during the process of reconstruction.

2.2   VISION AND OBJECTIVES

2.2.1.   The RDP links reconstruction and development in a process that will lead to growth in all parts of the economy, greater equity through redistribution, and sustainability. The RDP is committed to a programme of sustainable development which addresses the needs of our people without compromising the interests of future generations. Without meeting basic needs, no political democracy can survive in South Africa. We cannot undo the effects of apartheid overnight, but an extreme sense of urgency is required because reconstruction and development are major thrusts of the National Peace Initiative.

2.2.2.   Attacking poverty and deprivation is the first priority of the democratic government, and the RDP sets out a facilitating and enabling environment to this end. The RDP addresses issues of social, institutional, environmental and macro-economic sustainability in an integrated manner, with specific attention to affordability. We acknowledge the crucial role of provincial and local governments in adopting and implementing what are described here mainly as national-level programmes to meet basic needs. The RDP is also based on the premise that user charges will take into account socio-economic circumstances.

2.2.3.   The central objective of our RDP is to improve the quality of life of all South Africans, and in particular the most poor and marginalised sections of our communities. This objective should be realised through a process of empowerment which gives the poor control over their lives and increases their ability to mobilise sufficient development resources, including from the democratic government where necessary. The RDP reflects a commitment to grassroots, bottom-up development which is owned and driven by communities and their representative organisations.

2.2.4.   The strategy for meeting basic needs rests on four pillars, namely:

2.2.4.1.   creating opportunities for all South Africans to develop to their full potential;

2.2.4.2.   boosting production and household income through job creation, productivity and efficiency, improving conditions of employment, and creating opportunities for all to sustain themselves through productive activity;

2.2.4.3.   improving living conditions through better access to basic physical and social services, health care, and education and training for urban and rural communities, and

2.2.4.4.   establishing a social security system and other safety nets to protect the poor, the disabled, the elderly and other vulnerable groups.

2.2.5.   Through these strategies the RDP aims to meet the basic needs of the South African population in an integrated manner, combining urban, peri-urban and rural development processes. The integration of the RDP strategies is explained in Chapter Four, 'Building the Economy'. Priority areas that are considered in the present chapter are job creation through public works programmes, and provision of a variety of basic needs:
• land reform
• housing and services
• water and sanitation
• energy and electrification
• telecommunications
• transport
• environment
• nutrition
• health care
• social security and social welfare
(The RDP objectives in education and training, arts and culture, sport and recreation, and youth development are elaborated in Chapter Three, 'Developing our Human Resources'.)

2.2.6.   A programme of affirmative action must address the deliberate marginalisation from economic, political and social power of black people, women, and rural communities. Within this programme particularly vulnerable groups such as farm workers, the elderly and the youth require targeted intervention.

2.2.7.   The role of women within the RDP requires particular emphasis. Women are the majority of the poor in South Africa. Mechanisms to address the disempowerment of women and boost their role within the development process and economy must be implemented. The RDP must recognise and address existing gender inequalities as they affect access to jobs, land, housing, etc.

2.2.8.   The issue of population growth must be put into perspective. The present population policy, which asserts that overpopulation is the cause of poverty, ignores the role of apartheid in creating poverty, and also implies that the population growth rate is escalating (which is untrue). It is true, however, that a relatively high population growth rate exacerbates the basic needs backlogs our society faces. Raising the standard of living of the entire society, through successful implementation of the RDP, is essential over the longer term if we are to achieve a lower population growth rate. In particular, the impact of any programme on the population growth rate must be considered. A population committee should be located within the national RDP implementing structure. Policies on international migration must be reassessed bearing in mind the long-term interests of all of the people of the sub-continent.

2.2.9.   The lack of accurate statistics to quantify and locate the problem of poverty underlines the need for a national unit to monitor poverty and deprivation in an ongoing manner, and guide further interventions. The unit must develop and evaluate key indicators for measuring the success of the RDP. It must pay special attention to women's legal, educational and employment status and the rates of infant and maternal mortality and teenage pregnancy. Indeed, monitoring and gathering of all statistical data must, where relevant, incorporate the status of women and their economic position with specific reference to race, income distribution, rural and urban specifics, provincial dimensions, and age particularities (for example, women pensioners and young women). It is also necessary to develop a more acute demographic map of our people, both as to where they are presently located and, more importantly, where they could move so as to facilitate supply of infrastructure and services.

2.2.10. The first democratic South African government should sign and implement the International Covenant on Economic, Cultural and Social Rights (and related conventions) and establish a domestic equivalent of a high-profile Covenant review committee and reporting procedure.

2.3 JOBS THROUGH PUBLIC WORKS

2.3.1. The democratic government must play a leading role in building an economy which offers to all South Africans the opportunity to contribute productively. All job creation programmes should cater particularly for women and youth. Implementing agencies should include representatives from women's and youth organisations. Further job creation policies are identified in Chapter Four, 'Building the Economy'.

2.3.2. In the short term, the RDP must generate programmes to address unemployment. These measures must be an integral part of the programme to build the economy, and must also relate to meeting basic needs.

2.3.3. Although a much stronger welfare system is needed to support all the vulnerable, the old, the disabled and the sick who currently live in poverty, a system of 'handouts' for the unemployed should be avoided. All South Africans should have the opportunity to participate in the economic life of the country.

2.3.4. All short-term job creation programmes must ensure adequate incomes and labour standards, link into local, regional or national development programmes, and promote education, training and community capacity and empowerment.

2.3.5. **Public works programme.** The key area where special measures to create jobs can link to building the economy and meeting basic needs is in redressing apartheid-created infrastructural disparities. There must be a coordinated national public works programme to provide much-needed infrastructure, to repair environmental damage, and to link back into, expand and contribute to the restructuring of the industrial and agricultural base.

2.3.6. A further component of the public works programme must be provision of education and training and the involvement of communities in the process so that they are empowered to contribute to their own governance. Assets created by a public works project must be technically sound.

2.3.7. The public works programme must maximise the involvement of women and youth in the poorest rural households and most deprived regions to create assets such as water supply, sanitation and clinics. This must have significant socio-economic benefits, particularly with respect to production which meets women's basic needs (such as child-care facilities).

2.3.8. The public works programme must coordinate with and link to other job creation and labour-intensive construction initiatives. A community development fund could be set up within the context of a national public works programme to make resources available to communities. Care must be taken to ensure that disbursements from such a fund are carefully controlled and relate to local and regional development plans.

2.3.9. A national coordinating agency located in the implementing office of the RDP must ensure that the public works programme is based on the capital programmes at central, provincial and local level, give priority to job creation and training, target the most marginalised sectors of society, and where possible encourage and support self-employment through small and medium enterprise creation to ensure sustainability of skills. Such programmes must not abuse labour standards nor create unfair competition within sectors of the economy.

2.4 LAND REFORM

2.4.1. Land is the most basic need for rural dwellers. Apartheid policies pushed millions of black South Africans into overcrowded and impoverished reserves, homelands and townships. In addition, capital-intensive agricultural policies led to the large-scale eviction of farm dwellers from their land and homes. The abolition of the Land Acts cannot redress inequities in land distribution. Only a tiny minority of black people can afford land on the free market.

2.4.2.   A national land reform programme is the central and driving force of a programme of rural development. Such a programme aims to address effectively the injustices of forced removals and the historical denial of access to land. It aims to ensure security of tenure for rural dwellers. And in implementing the national land reform programme, and through the provision of support services, the democratic government will build the economy by generating large-scale employment, increasing rural incomes and eliminating overcrowding.

2.4.3.   The RDP must implement a fundamental land reform programme. This programme must be demand-driven and must aim to supply residential and productive land to the poorest section of the rural population and aspirant farmers. As part of a comprehensive rural development programme, it must raise incomes and productivity, and must encourage the use of land for agricultural, other productive, or residential purposes.

2.4.4.   The land policy must ensure security of tenure for all South Africans, regardless of their system of land-holding. It must remove all forms of discrimination in women's access to land.

2.4.5.   The land reform programme has two aspects: **redistribution** of residential and productive land to those who need it but cannot afford it, and **restitution** for those who lost land because of apartheid laws.

2.4.6.   **Land redistribution.** The land redistribution programme will realise its objectives in various ways, including strengthening property rights of communities already occupying land, combining market and non-market mechanisms to provide land, and using vacant government land.

2.4.7.   The redistribution programme should use land already on sale and land acquired by corrupt means from the apartheid state or mortgaged to state and parastatal bodies. Where applicable, it will expropriate land and pay compensation as the Constitution stipulates. Land acquired from the apartheid state through illegal means must be recovered after due process of investigation. The land reform programme must include land outside of the historically black areas. All legal provisions which may impede the planning and affordability of a land reform programme must be reviewed and if necessary revised.

2.4.8. The democratic government must provide substantial funding for land redistribution. In addition, beneficiaries must pay in accordance with their means. A land tax on rural land must be based on clear criteria, must help to free up underutilised land, must raise revenues for rural infrastructure, and must promote the productive use of land.

2.4.9. Rural infrastructure, support services and training at all levels must be provided to ensure that land can be utilised effectively. Within this, water provision must take priority, followed by provision of basic health care. To this end a safe rural water supply programme must begin in the first year of the RDP.

2.4.10. A democratic government must ensure secure tenure rights for all South Africans by adopting a tenure policy that recognises the diverse forms of tenure existing in South Africa. It must support the development of new and innovative forms of tenure such as Community Land Trusts and other forms of group land-holding.

2.4.11. Women face specific disabilities in obtaining land. The land redistribution programme must therefore target women. Institutions, practices and laws that discriminate against women's access to land must be reviewed and brought in line with national policy. In particular, tenure and matrimonial laws must be revised appropriately.

2.4.12. The programme must include the provision of services to beneficiaries of land reform so that they can use their land as productively as possible. Assistance must include support for local institution building, so that communities can devise equitable and effective ways to allocate and administer land.

2.4.13. **Land restitution.** To redress the suffering caused by the policy of forced removals, the democratic government must, through the mechanism of a land claims court, restore land to South Africans dispossessed by discriminatory legislation since 1913. This court must be accessible to the poor and illiterate. It must establish processes that enable it to take speedy decisions. In order for this court to function effectively, constitutional rights to restitution must be guaranteed.

2.4.14. The land reform programme, including costing, implementing mechanisms, and a training programme, must be in place within one year after the elections. The programme must aim to redistribute 30 per cent of agricultural land within the first five years of the programme. The land restitution programme must aim to complete its task of adjudication in five years.

2.5 HOUSING AND SERVICES

2.5.1. The lack of adequate housing and basic services in urban townships and rural settlements today has reached crisis proportions. The urban housing backlog in 1990 was conservatively estimated at 1,3 million units. Including hostels and rural areas, the backlog rises to approximately three million units. To this should be added an estimated 200 000 new households each year. There is, unfortunately, little research available on the rural housing situation and the bantustans.

2.5.2. About 50 000 houses were built in South Africa in 1992. This figure could reasonably be increased to over 300 000 units each year by the end of the RDP's five-year programme. At minimum, one million low-cost houses should be constructed over five years. These units should be specifically intended for low-income households and should include the rural areas.

2.5.3. The housing problems created by apartheid and by the limited range of the capitalist housing markets have been aggravated by the absence of a coherent national housing policy. A mass housing programme can help generate employment, skills and economic activity, both directly and indirectly, and should help ensure peace and stability. A single national housing department should help to consolidate the previously fragmented approach. The private sector and civil society also have important roles to play in expanding housing delivery and financing capacity. The development of small, medium-sized and micro enterprises owned and run by black people must be incorporated into the housing delivery programme.

2.5.4. **Right to housing.** The RDP endorses the principle that all South Africans have a right to a secure place in which to live in peace and dignity. Housing is a human right. One of the RDP's first priorities is to provide for the homeless.

2.5.5. Although housing may be provided by a range of parties, the democratic government is ultimately responsible for ensuring that housing is provided to all. It must create a policy framework and legislative support so that this is possible, and it must allocate subsidy funds from the budget – to reach a goal of not less than five per cent of the budget by the end of the five-year RDP – so that housing is affordable to even the poorest South Africans.

2.5.6. The approach to housing, infrastructure and services must involve and empower communities; be affordable, developmental and sustainable; take account of funding and resource constraints, and support gender equality. The RDP is committed to establishing viable communities in areas close to economic opportunities and to health, educational, social amenities and transport infrastructure.

2.5.7. **Housing standards.** As a minimum, all housing must provide protection from weather, a durable structure, and reasonable living space and privacy. A house must include sanitary facilities, storm-water drainage, a household energy supply (whether linked to grid electricity supply or derived from other sources, such as solar energy), and convenient access to clean water. Moreover, it must provide for secure tenure in a variety of forms. Upgrading of existing housing must be accomplished with these minimum standards in mind.

2.5.8.   Community organisations and other stakeholders must establish minimum basic standards for housing types, construction, planning and development, for both units and communities. Legislation must also be introduced to establish appropriate housing construction standards, although such standards should not preclude more detailed provisions negotiated at local level.

2.5.9.   **Legislation.** Legislation must be rapidly developed to address issues such as tenants' rights, squatters' rights, the rights of people living in informal settlements, community reinvestment by banks, evictions, consumer protection, land restoration, community participation in planning and development, and anti-discrimination protection. Exploitation in rentals charged and in quality of housing provided must be specifically legislated against. All legislative obstacles and constraints to housing and credit for women must be removed. The democratic government must promote and facilitate women's access to housing and to appropriate community design. The provision of appropriate housing for the elderly and the disabled is also an important priority.

2.5.10. **Administration.** Administrative procedures must be simple, cheap, quick, transparent, must support community participation and must prevent corruption, with no form of discrimination of any kind whatsoever.

2.5.11. **Land.** Land for housing must be suitably located geologically, environmentally, and with respect to economic opportunities and social amenities. The democratic government must intervene to facilitate access to such land. Land speculation must be prevented and land monopolies broken up. Land planning must involve the communities affected. Land taxes and zoning should seek to promote urban development patterns consistent with RDP objectives.

2.5.12. **Tenure.** The democratic government must ensure a wide range of tenure options including individual and collective home ownership as well as rental, and facilitate a wide range of housing types. Sufficient affordable rental housing stock should be provided to low-income earners who choose this option.

2.5.13.   The democratic government must support the transfer
of houses to those who have been denied the
opportunity to own houses in the past, especially
female heads of household. The transfer of houses to
long-term residents, as has been negotiated, must be
completed. Fees charged by the democratic government
for the transfer of private housing must be made more
affordable.

2.5.14.   **Subsidies.** Government funds and private sector
funding must be blended in order to make housing
finance affordable. A national housing bank and
national home loan guarantee fund must be initiated to
coordinate subsidies and financing most efficiently.
Subsidies must be provided in ways which reduce
corruption, promote transparency, target the poor and
eliminate gender discrimination. Mechanisms (such as
time limits on resale, or compulsory repayment of
subsidies upon transfer of property) must be introduced
to prevent speculation and downward raiding. Subsidies
could apply to a variety of tenure forms, but must be
paid directly to individuals, groups or community-
controlled institutions. Communities must get sufficient
funds in order to ensure that they are not divided.

2.5.15.   **Finance.** End-user finance and credit must be made
available for diverse tenure forms, community designs
and housing construction methods. Commercial banks
must be encouraged, through legislation and incentives,
to make credit and other services available in low-
income areas; 'redlining' and other forms of
discrimination by banks must be prohibited. Community-
controlled financing vehicles must be established with
both private sector and government support where
necessary. Locally controlled Housing Associations or
cooperatives must be supported, in part to take over
properties in possession of banks due to foreclosure.
Unemployment bond insurance packages and
guarantee schemes with a demand-side orientation
must be devised. Interest rates must be kept as low as
possible.

2.5.16.   **Hostels.** Hostels must be transformed, upgraded and
integrated within a policy framework that recognises
the numerous interest groups in and around hostels and
provides a range of housing options, including both

family units and single people. The transformation of hostels must not deny any individuals or households access to the cities, including workers who maintain a rural base, families who desire integration into the city, and women with no security. Policies must address integration of hostels into communities, their safety and privacy (especially for women and children), and the various family living arrangements in hostels. Migrant labour, a consequence of past recruitment policies, will persist in the immediate future. Some housing types should be developed to cater for migrant workers and for those who engage in circular migration between city and countryside. Privately-owned hostels must be given particular attention. Short-term repairs (including provision of basic services and a baseline healthy environment) are a first priority, but must be consistent with long-term transformation. A fundamental point of departure is affordability. The democratic government must upgrade hostels where residents cannot pay costs. Hostels programmes must put appropriate dispute resolution mechanisms in place, must be linked to programmes for the unemployed, and address the legacy of migrant labour.

2.5.17. **Rural housing.** Rural people have specific concerns around housing, such as tenure forms on trust land; the relationship with the commercial agricultural sector; inadequate or non-existent bulk infrastructure; farm workers housed on the farms; the legacy of apartheid removals and resettlements; access to land, and land claims procedures and processes. In rural areas, problems of ensuring full property and home-ownership rights for women are likely to be greater. A rural housing action plan must be developed to address this. While recognising that rural incomes are far lower, the democratic government must consider rural housing needs in calculating backlogs, and make provision for gradually improving housing in rural areas. In particular, labour tenants require security of tenure, and legal defence and advice offices must be established to assist farm workers in cases of eviction.

2.5.18. **Role players.** All actors in the housing sector must be identified and their roles clearly defined, to enable coordinated and efficient housing provision. Role players include civic associations and other community groups, the public sector, non-governmental organisations, private sector developers and construction materials firms, trade unions, financial institutions, etc. The work of the National Housing Forum should be encouraged to continue, but there must be effective public sector participation as well. Duplication, inefficiency and ineffectiveness must be eliminated.

2.5.19. **Construction.** The costs of housing construction must be kept as low as possible while meeting the proposed standards. Bulk-buying facilities and other support mechanisms must be introduced in order to maximise use of local materials and to develop products that lower costs and increase the efficiency of housing provision. The building materials industries must be examined, both to improve productive output and to reduce costs. Cartels, price agreements and market share agreements must end, and consideration must be given to public, worker and community-based ownership where the market fails to provide a reasonably priced product. Community-controlled building materials suppliers must be encouraged, possibly with government subsidies to enhance competitiveness. An enforceable Code of Conduct must be established to guide developers. Special funds must be made available to support small and medium-sized enterprises. Resources should be provided in the form of loans for bridging finance, and grants for training and entrepreneurial development.

2.5.20. **Delivery.** Delivery systems will depend upon community participation. While the central government has financing responsibilities, provincial and local governments should be the primary agencies facilitating the delivery of housing and should be particularly active in the delivery of rental housing stock. Organisations of civil society should play a supportive role in relation to local government to enhance the delivery process. The roles of various entities in the private sector (the construction and supplies industry, etc.), local business concerns, local cooperatives and the concept of self-build in the delivery of housing must be examined in the light of effectiveness and local benefit. Delivery systems should aim to maximise job creation, the use of local materials, and local income generation and training. Support must be provided to black and, more generally, to small builders.

2.5.21. **Community control.** Beneficiary communities should be involved at all levels of decision-making and in the implementation of their projects. Communities should benefit directly from programmes in matters such as employment, training and award of contracts. Key to such participation is capacity building, and funds for community-based organisations must be made available. Educational institutions must also be reorientated to provide the skills needed for development.

2.6 WATER AND SANITATION

2.6.1. Water is a natural resource, and should be made available in a sustainable manner to all South Africans. Today, more than 12 million people do not have access to clean drinking water and 21 million people do not have adequate sanitation (toilets and refuse removal). Less than half the rural population has a safe and accessible water supply, and only one person in seven has access to adequate sanitation. Communities have had little say in the provision of water and sanitation, and decision-making in the water delivery agencies has reflected broader apartheid ideology. Access to water resources is dominated by a privileged minority while the majority of the population enjoy little or no water security.

2.6.2. South Africa is a water-scarce country. The existing limited water resources are also unevenly distributed, with 70 per cent of the country receiving 11 per cent of the rainfall. Apartheid South Africa used its military and economic might to coerce its neighbours into acting as sources of water, sometimes to the detriment of these countries' own water needs and of the sub-continental watertable.

2.6.3. **Right to water.** The fundamental principle of our water resources policy is the right to access clean water – 'water security for all'. The RDP recognises the economic value of water and the environment, and advocates an economically, environmentally and politically sustainable approach to the management of our water resources and the collection, treatment and disposal of waste.

2.6.4. Because of geographic limits to the availability of water, there must be very careful attention paid to the location of new settlements. The long-term environmental costs of sourcing water from neighbouring countries and between provinces must be given greater consideration. South Africa is also a drought-prone country, and a national drought management system and water reserves are a priority.

2.6.5. **Goals of water management.** Water management has three main goals: meeting every person's health and functional requirements, raising agricultural output, and supporting economic development. Decisions on water resources must be transparent and justified so as to reduce conflict between competing users. The use of water must be balanced with a realisation of the dangers of overuse and inappropriate disposal. Community organisations must also receive training in water management and must ensure such management is integrated into overall planning.

2.6.6. The RDP's short-term aim is to provide every person with adequate facilities for health. The RDP will achieve this by establishing a national water and sanitation programme which aims to provide all households with a clean, safe water supply of 20 – 30 litres per capita per day (lcd) within 200 metres, an adequate/safe sanitation facility per site, and a refuse removal system to all urban households.

2.6.7. In the medium term, the RDP aims to provide an on-site supply of 50 – 60 lcd of clean water, improved on-site sanitation, and an appropriate household refuse collection system. Water supply to nearly 100 per cent of rural households should be achieved over the medium term, and adequate sanitation facilities should be provided to at least 75 per cent of rural households. Community/household preferences and environmental sustainability will be taken into account.

2.6.8. The RDP's long-term goal is to provide every South African with accessible water and sanitation.

2.6.9.   The RDP is committed to providing operation and maintenance systems which ensure minimum disruptions in service within two years. Particularly in rural areas, the RDP must develop appropriate institutions, including village water committees. Consultation with communities is essential in the provision of water.

2.6.10.   **Tariffs.** To ensure that every person has an adequate water supply, the national tariff structure must include the following:

2.6.10.1.   a lifeline tariff to ensure that all South Africans are able to afford water services sufficient for health and hygiene requirements;

2.6.10.2.   in urban areas, a progressive block tariff to ensure that the long-term costs of supplying large-volume users are met and that there is a cross-subsidy to promote affordability for the poor, and

2.6.10.3.   in rural areas, a tariff that covers operating and maintenance costs of services, and recovery of capital costs from users on the basis of a cross-subsidy from urban areas in cases of limited rural affordability.

2.6.11.   The following institutions must be restructured:

2.6.11.1.   the Department of Water Affairs should be responsible for the integrated management of the nation's water resources for the benefit of the whole nation, and should take responsibility for building competent local and provincial agencies that are capable of delivery;

2.6.11.2.   at a second tier, water resource management must be founded on catchment-based institutions to ensure effective control over and supply of water resources, as well as effective management of and control over waste water, which means that the boundaries of such institutions will not

necessarily coincide with provincial
boundaries, and

2.6.11.3.   at local level, local governments must be
made responsible for water distribution,
provision of adequate sanitation facilities
and waste removal, and the financing of
these services through appropriate tariff and
local tax mechanisms.

2.6.12.   The RDP must undertake a process to involve all
relevant parties in updating the Water Act to ensure
the right of all South Africans to water security.

2.6.13.   South Africa has several major river systems which are
shared with neighbouring countries. Since there is likely
to be a need to import water from other countries, a
future democratic government must pursue a policy of
mutual cooperation with its neighbours and create
bilateral and multilateral treaties which ensure the fair
and adequate allocation of water resources to the
benefit of the people of the region as a whole.

2.7   ENERGY AND ELECTRIFICATION

2.7.1.   Although energy is a basic need and a vital input into
the informal sector, the vast majority of South African
households and entrepreneurs depend on inferior and
expensive fuels. Rural women in particular face a heavy
burden collecting wood which is an inefficient and
unhealthy fuel. Urban households face high costs for
paraffin and gas. Coal, where it is available, is cheap
but results in severe health problems, an underpaid
workforce, and the failure to assess and internalise
environmental costs. Although Eskom has excess
generating capacity, only 36 per cent of South African
households have access to electricity, leaving some
three million households unelectrified. Furthermore,
some 19 000 black schools (86 per cent) and around
4 000 clinics are currently without electricity. Little
attention has been paid to utilising sustainable energy
sources such as solar power.

2.7.2.   The control of electricity distribution by the system of
racially separate local government has resulted in a

terribly fragmented industry currently unable to finance or sustain a large-scale electrification programme in an equitable fashion. At present there are around 430 electricity distributors and more than 1 000 domestic electricity tariffs in South Africa. Rural electrification has been largely ignored except for commercial white farms.

2.7.3. Past South African energy policies concentrated on achieving energy self-sufficiency at enormous cost (such as the Mossgas project), but seriously neglected the household sector. Future energy policy must concentrate on the provision of energy services to meet the basic needs of poor households, stimulate productive capacity and urgently meet the energy needs associated with community services such as schools, clinics and water supplies. Energy policies must be developed on the basis of an integration of supply-side and demand-side considerations.

2.7.4. **Energy sources.** Immediate policies to meet energy needs must include a low-smoke coal programme, improved management of natural woodlands, social forestry programmes, commercial woodlots, and support for the transport of wood from areas of surplus to areas of need. Gas and paraffin prices must be reduced through better regulation and by bringing bulk supplies closer to households.

2.7.5. Energy efficiency and conservation must be a cornerstone of energy policies. This will involve the adoption of least-cost planning approaches; the improvement of dwelling thermal performance; the promotion of energy-efficient appliances; the use of solar water heaters; appliance labelling, and the implementation of time-of-use electricity tariffs. Financial assistance to ensure households have access to efficient appliances will be essential. The environmental impact of different energy sources must be assessed.

2.7.6. The regulation of liquid fuels is necessary to ensure a stable, high-quality supply, stable investment and low input prices to the economy and consumers.

2.7.7.   **Electricity for all.** An accelerated and sustainable electrification programme must provide access to electricity for an additional 2,5 million households by the year 2000, thereby increasing the level of access to electricity to about 72 per cent of all households (double the present number). Both grid and non-grid power sources (such as solar cells and generators) must be employed. All schools and clinics must be electrified as soon as possible. Communities must be involved in the planning and execution of this programme. Micro, small and medium-sized enterprises must be given support and shown preference in the tendering process.

2.7.8.   The electrification programme will cost around R12 billion with annual investments peaking at R2 billion. This must be financed from within the industry as far as possible via cross-subsidies from other electricity consumers. Where necessary the democratic government will provide concessionary finance for the electrification of poor households in remote rural areas. A national Electrification Fund, underwritten by a government guarantee, must be created to raise bulk finance from lenders and investors for electrification. Such a fund could potentially be linked to a Reconstruction Fund to be utilised for other related infrastructural financing needs. A national domestic tariff structure with low connection fees must be established to promote affordability.

2.7.9.   **Energy Policy Council.** A national Energy Policy Council should be established to bring together stakeholders including the government, unions, civics, the energy industries, and consumers. This Energy Policy Council should manage the Electrification Fund and formulate energy policies.

2.7.10.   Until the formation of the Energy Policy Council the National Electricity Forum must continue to work towards agreement on the restructuring of the fragmented electricity industry. To assist with this a powerful, independent, national electricity regulator must be established to enforce public policy, ensure long-term financial viability, assure environmental sustainability, and act as an ombuds in the event of conflicts between consumers, government and the electricity industry.

2.8 TELECOMMUNICATIONS

2.8.1.   Telecommunications is an information infrastructure and must play a crucial role in South Africa's health, education, agricultural, informal sector, policing and safety programmes. Under apartheid the provision of telecommunications was racially distorted. For black people it is estimated that less than 1 line per 100 persons is in place compared with about 60 lines per 100 white persons. Other countries with comparable per capita wealth have 30 lines per 100 persons. The situation is far worse in rural areas.

2.8.2.   The existing parastatal Telkom is restricted by heavy debt from engaging in substantial further borrowing, and an indiscriminate privatisation process has fragmented the telecommunications system. The lack of infrastructure has also restricted the provision of services to peri-urban and rural areas. Other telecommunications networks are not well integrated into the existing Telkom network.

2.8.3.   The telecommunications sector is an indispensable backbone for the development of all other socio-economic sectors. An effective telecommunications infrastructure which includes universal access is essential to enable the delivery of basic services and the reconstruction and development of deprived areas.

2.8.4.   The RDP aims to provide universal affordable access for all as rapidly as possible within a sustainable and viable telecommunications system; to develop a modern and integrated telecommunications and information technology system that is capable of enhancing, cheapening and facilitating education, health care, business information, public administration and rural development, and to develop a Southern African cooperative programme for telecommunications. In terms of the RDP, telecommunications services must be provided to all schools and clinics within two years.

2.9 TRANSPORT

2.9.1. The policy of apartheid has moved the poor away from job opportunities and access to amenities. This has burdened the workforce with enormous travel distances to their places of employment and commercial centres, and thus with excessive costs. Apartheid transport policy deprived the majority of people of a say in transport matters, and has led to the payment of huge travel subsidies; exposed commuters to vast walking distances and insecure rail travel; failed to regulate the kombi-taxi industry adequately; largely ignored the country's outrageous road safety record; paid little attention to the environmental impact of transport projects, and facilitated transport decision-making bodies that are unwieldy, unfocused, unaccountable and bureaucratic.

2.9.2. Rural areas require more frequent public transport and improved facilities, at an affordable cost. There is inadequate access for emergency services in rural areas, inadequate public transport frequencies and route coverage, poor coordination, and other inefficiencies. Indeed, in many rural areas there is no public transport at all.

2.9.3. An effective publicly-owned passenger transport system must be developed, integrating road, rail and air transportation. All privately-controlled passenger transport must be effectively regulated and controlled. A future transport policy must:

   2.9.3.1. promote coordinated, safe, affordable public transport as a social service;

   2.9.3.2. be flexible enough to take cognisance of local conditions in order to make best use of the available transport infrastructure;

   2.9.3.3. ensure accountability so that the people have control over what is provided;

   2.9.3.4. take into account the transport needs of disabled people;

2.9.3.5.   clearly define the responsibilities of the various authorities;

2.9.3.6.   ensure comprehensive land-use/transport planning;

2.9.3.7.   promote road safety;

2.9.3.8.   review subsidies (both operating and capital);

2.9.3.9.   provide funds for long-term planning, and

2.9.3.10. facilitate high-density development to ensure efficient use of public transport.

2.9.4.   As population increases, the numbers of travellers and the total distances travelled will also increase. The majority will be unable to afford private transport and will be dependent upon public transport. Given the need for increased mobility and the cost and environmental impact of accommodating the private motorist, the future emphasis must be on the provision of safe, convenient, affordable public transport.

2.9.5.   **Public transport.** Commuters should be encouraged to use public transport, and should be actively discouraged from using cars (via parking, access and fuel levies). The funds so raised must be used to directly benefit the provision of public transport. As a first priority, rail transport must be extended. Bus lines must act as feeders to rail services, or as prime movers if rail is not available. Taxis must act as feeders to bus/rail services or as prime movers if neither rail nor bus is available. The subsidisation of parallel services along a common route will be avoided. Rural areas require more frequent public transport and improved facilities, at affordable costs.

2.9.6.   At the same time, critical 'bottlenecks' in the road infrastructure should be improved so that the full capacity of the existing road network can be realised. However, the provision of primary road infrastructure must be directed towards and take cognisance of public transport needs.

2.9.7.   **Transport planning.** The planning of transport for metropolitan and major urban areas must be in accordance with an urban/metropolitan growth management plan. A hierarchy of modes should guide the financing of infrastructure improvements and payment of operating subsidies for public transport. Travel modes should not compete. In rural areas, provincial governments and district councils must present transport plans, including extensive road building and road improvement.

2.9.8.   South Africa has the worst road safety record in the world. Central government funds allocated to ameliorate this situation via education, enforcement and engineering have been negligible. Road safety must be given the priority it deserves. The transport authorities must be charged with the task of reducing accidents and must be given the funds to achieve that goal.

2.9.9.   For all public transport services to be fully integrated their functioning must be coordinated and financed by one organisation. The organisation should be accountable to the public and responsible for the provision, coordination and funding of all public transport and the infrastructure necessary for public transport (in cooperation with the national public works programme). The organisation should specifically address current problems such as uncoordinated tariff structures, duplication of services, and conflict as a result of different forms of ownership. Minimum norms and standards, policy frameworks and the format of transport plans for national, provincial, urban and rural areas should form an integral part of the responsibilities of this organisation.

2.9.10. Provincial governments should be responsible for the provision and coordination of all primary inter-city transport outside the metropolitan areas and, on request, for localised, minor improvements for towns and villages beyond metropolitan areas.

2.9.11. Metropolitan Transport Authorities (MTAs) should be responsible for planning, coordination and provision of all 'metropolitan' transport facilities within metro areas. The MTAs could undertake local authority projects on an agency basis. The MTAs must be accountable to democratically elected metropolitan governments, and all transport projects must be in accord with metropolitan plans. Funding for public transport would come both from central government and from local rates and taxes. The MTAs must be empowered to impose such levies and taxes as may be appropriate and the funds thus raised must be used primarily to promote public transport.

2.9.12. With respect to other forms of transport, international conventions and treaties will determine part of the legal framework in which sea and air transport develop. Infrastructural development must, however, be extended through democratic consultations with various stakeholders. Harmonisation of infrastructural, legal and operational aspects of regional Southern African transport must be considered a priority.

2.9.13. The needs of women, children, and disabled people for affordable and safe transport are important. Adequate public transport at off-peak hours, and security measures on late-night and isolated routes, must be provided. Additional subsidies for scholars, pensioners and others with limited incomes will be considered.

2.10 ENVIRONMENT

2.10.1. Apartheid legislation distorted access to natural resources, denying the majority of South Africans the use of land, water, fisheries, minerals, wildlife and clean air. South Africa's apartheid policies, combined with the underregulated activities of local and transnational corporations, contributed to the degradation of environmental resources, including soil, water and vegetation. They encouraged the misuse of fertilisers and pesticides. They placed workers' lives at severe risk because dangerous practices and substances were inadequately monitored (mining in South Africa remains an extremely dangerous job). Poverty and environmental degradation have been closely linked. In general, existing environmental policies allow inefficient and wasteful use of water, energy and raw materials, and high levels of air and water pollution.

2.10.2.   The democratic government must ensure that all South African citizens, present and future, have the right to a decent quality of life through sustainable use of resources. To achieve this, the government must work towards:

2.10.2.1.   equitable access to natural resources;

2.10.2.2.   safe and healthy living and working environments, and

2.10.2.3.   a participatory decision-making process around environmental issues, empowering communities to manage their natural environment.

2.10.3.   Environmental considerations must be built into every decision. To accomplish this, procedures must be set in place which oblige decision-makers to demonstrate what environmental considerations they take into account when considering projects.

2.10.4.   Development strategies must incorporate environmental consequences in the course of planning. Measures such as land reform, provision of basic infrastructure, housing and targeted rural assistance (including extension services), and the maintenance of food security should ultimately reduce pressure on the natural environment.

2.10.5.   The democratic government must revise current environmental legislation and administration with a view to establishing an effective system of environmental management. It must make use of environmental auditing, with provision for public disclosure. It must monitor those activities of industry which impact on the environment.

2.10.6.   Strategies should include:

2.10.6.1.   a system of waste management with emphasis on preventing pollution and reducing waste through direct controls, and on increasing the capacity of citizens and government to monitor and prevent the dumping of toxic wastes;

2.10.6.2. participation of communities in management and decision-making in wildlife conservation and the related tourism benefits;

2.10.6.3. environmental education programmes to rekindle our people's love for the land, to increase environmental consciousness amongst our youth, to coordinate environmental education with education policy at all levels, and to empower communities to act on environmental issues and to promote an environmental ethic, and

2.10.6.4. the establishment of procedures, rights and duties to allow workers to monitor the effects of pollution, noise levels and dangerous practices both within the workplace and in its impact on surrounding communities and environment.

2.10.7. Marine resources must be managed and controlled for the benefit of all South Africans, especially those communities whose livelihood depends on resources from the sea. The fishing stock must be managed in a way that promotes sustainable yield and the development of new species. The democratic government must assist people to have access to these resources. Legislative measures must be introduced to establish democratic structures for the management of sea resources.

2.10.8. **Environmental regulation.** South Africa has wide-ranging environmental legislation. However, responsibility for implementation is scattered over a number of departments (Agriculture, Water Affairs and Forestry, Health, and Mineral Resources) from national to local authority level. The Department of Environmental Affairs administers only a few of the relevant Acts. This has resulted in discrepancies, anomalies and ineffectiveness.

2.10.9. Fines for environmental offences are inadequate and inconsistent. The South African legal system makes it difficult to obtain *locus standi* in the courts on environmental issues.

2.10.10. The democratic government must rationalise environmental legislation into a cohesive and workable form. It must legislate the right of access to information on environmentally harmful practices. It must also require compulsory environmental impact assessments for all large-scale projects. It must establish an environmental ombuds and criminalise environmental offences. It must review and conform with international conventions and agreements on environmental issues.

2.10.11. Environmental management must be transformed to promote the active participation of civil society.

2.10.12. Both local and provincial governments must play a crucial role in environmental management. Strong provincial departments of Environmental Affairs must be established. A national Department of Environmental Affairs must ensure overall standards and financing of environmental protection.

2.10.13. A Commission on the Environment must be established as an independent body to ensure transparency and accountability on the part of agencies dealing with the environment. Such a body must facilitate the gathering, collation and publication of data on the environment. It must also provide an interface between civil society and public agencies responsible for the environment and natural resources.

2.11 NUTRITION

2.11.1. An enormous number of South African children under the age of 10 years are malnourished and/or stunted. Many thousands of adults, especially the elderly, are hungry, and millions of people, young and old, live in constant fear of being hungry.

2.11.2. The RDP must ensure that as soon as possible, and certainly within three years, every person in South Africa can get their basic nutritional requirement each day and that they no longer live in fear of going hungry.

2.11.3. The most important step toward food security remains the provision of productive employment opportunities through land reform, jobs programmes and the reorganisation of the economy.

2.11.4. Short-term interventions should support nutrition education and the stable, low-cost supply of staple foods combined with carefully targeted income transfers and food subsidies.

2.11.5. The democratic government must ensure that VAT is not applied to basic foodstuffs, improve social security payments and reintroduce price controls on standard bread. It must enhance the efficiency of marketing so that farmers receive good prices while consumers pay as little as possible. To that end, the government should curb the powers of marketing boards and monopolies, and review the effect of tariffs.

2.11.6. The democratic government should institute a National Nutrition Surveillance System, which should aim to weigh a statistically significant proportion of children under the age of five years each month to establish their levels of growth and wellbeing. These simple data will provide measures of food security in each area, measures which are essential both for health planning and for targeting relief, for instance during drought. More widely, South Africa currently lacks an early warning system which can alert central authorities to threats to food and water security. The RDP should establish institutions to collect and monitor nutritional and other key socio-economic and agricultural data.

2.12 HEALTH CARE

2.12.1. The mental, physical and social health of South Africans has been severely damaged by apartheid policies and their consequences. The health care and social services that have developed are grossly inefficient and inadequate. There are, by international standards, probably enough nurses, doctors and hospital beds. South Africa spends R550 per capita per annum on health care. This is nearly 10 times what the World Bank estimates it should cost to provide basic public health services and essential clinical care for all, yet millions of our people are without such services or such care. Health services are fragmented, inefficient and ineffective, and resources are grossly mismanaged and poorly distributed. The situation in rural areas is particularly bad.

2.12.2. This section of the RDP draws attention to a number of programmes designed to restructure the health care services in South Africa. The aim is to ensure that all South Africans get infinitely better value for the money spent in this area, and that their mental, physical and social health improves both for its own sake and as a major contribution to increasing prosperity and the quality of life for all.

2.12.3. A fundamental objective of the RDP is to raise the standard of living through improved wages and income-earning opportunities, and to improve sanitation, water supply, energy sources, and accommodation. All of this will have a positive impact on health. Many other policies and programmes affect health, and their implications should be explored and considered.

2.12.4. All policies affecting health must take into consideration the fact that South Africa is an integral part of the Southern African region and has regional responsibilities to prevent and to combat the spread of disease.

2.12.5. **National Health System (NHS).**

2.12.5.1. One of the first priorities is to draw all the different role players and services into the NHS. This must include both public and private providers of goods and services and must be organised at national, provincial, district and community levels.

2.12.5.2. Reconstruction in the health sector will involve the complete transformation of the entire delivery system. All relevant legislation, organisations and institutions must be reviewed in order to redress the harmful effects of apartheid; encourage and develop delivery systems and practices that are in line with international norms and standards; introduce management practices that promote efficient and compassionate delivery of services, and ensure respect for human rights and accountability to users, clients and the public at large.

2.12.5.3. Communities must be encouraged to participate actively in the planning, managing, delivery, monitoring and evaluation of the health services in their areas.

2.12.5.4. There must be a single Minister of Health and a single National Health Authority (NHA). The NHA must develop national policies, standards, norms and targets, allocate the health budget, coordinate the recruitment, training, distribution and conditions of service of health workers, and develop and implement a National Health Information System.

2.12.5.5. Each province must have a Provincial Health Authority (PHA). This PHA must be responsible for providing support to all the District Health Authorities (DHAs) in its province. This must include providing secondary and tertiary referral hospitals, regulating private hospitals, running training facilities and programmes, evaluating and planning services, and any other support the districts may request. The aim is to encourage high-quality, efficient services through decentralised management and local accountability.

2.12.5.6. The main bodies responsible for ensuring access to and the delivery of health services must be the DHAs. Each DHA must be responsible for the health of between 200 000 and 750 000 people in a defined geographical area. About 100 DHAs will, between them, cover the whole country and their boundaries must, as far as possible, be the same as the new local government boundaries. Each DHA will be responsible for all primary health care services in its district, including independent general practitioners and community hospitals. The DHA must have as much control over its budget as possible, within national and provincial guidelines.

2.12.5.7. In the first phase of the RDP the government must develop at least one model or pilot health district in each province. Each DHA must appoint a team, led by a District Health Manager and linked to a District Development Committee, to evaluate, plan and manage health services in the district, including management of the district health budget. The system must encourage the training, use and support of community health workers as cost-effective additional or alternative personnel.

2.12.5.8. The whole NHS must be driven by the Primary Health Care (PHC) approach. This emphasises community participation and empowerment, inter-sectoral collaboration and cost-effective care, as well as integration of preventive, promotive, curative and rehabilitation services.

2.12.5.9. All providers of health services must be accountable to the local communities they serve through a system of community committees and through the DHAs which must be part of democratically elected local government. Other strategies must include a charter of patients' rights that will be displayed in all health facilities; a Code of Conduct for health workers; a programme to promote gender balance in all categories of health workers; restructuring statutory bodies; support and supervision of staff at peripheral facilities and inter-sectoral structures at district, provincial and national levels.

2.12.5.10. Once statutory bodies have been rationalised and restructured to reflect the rich diversity of the South African people, they should be better able to promote and protect standards of training and of health care, and to protect the rights and interests of patients and clients.

2.12.6. **Women and children.**

2.12.6.1. Health care for all children under six years of age, and for all homeless children, must immediately be provided free at government clinics and health centres.

2.12.6.2. There must be a programme to improve maternal and child health through access to quality antenatal, delivery and postnatal services for all women. This must include better transport facilities and in-service training programmes for midwives and for traditional birth attendants. Targets must include 90 per cent of pregnant women receiving antenatal care and 75 per cent of deliveries being supervised and carried out under hygienic conditions within two years. By 1999, 90 per cent of deliveries should be supervised. These services must be free at government facilities by the third year of the RDP. In addition, there should be established the right to six months paid maternity leave and 10 days paternity leave.

2.12.6.3. Preventive and promotive health programmes for children must be improved. Breast-feeding must be encouraged and promoted, and the code of ethics on breast-milk substitutes enforced. A more effective, expanded programme of immunisation must achieve a coverage of 90 per cent within three years. Polio and neonatal tetanus can be eradicated within two years.

2.12.6.4. One important aspect of people being able to take control of their lives is their capacity to control their own fertility. The government must ensure that appropriate information and services are available to enable all people to do this. Reproductive rights must be guaranteed and reproductive health services must promote people's right to privacy and dignity. Every woman must have the right to choose whether or not to have an early termination of pregnancy according to her own individual beliefs. Reproductive rights must include education, counselling and confidentiality.

2.12.7. **Mental and psychological health.**

2.12.7.1. Millions of South Africans abuse alcohol, tobacco, cannabis (dagga), solvents like petrol and glue, and other harder drugs. Unless action is taken, substance abuse is likely to increase enormously. Abuse of these substances causes immense physical, mental and social damage and costs the country millions of rands each year. The RDP must aim to reduce greatly the present levels of substance abuse and to prevent any increase. Comprehensive strategies to change behaviour must include education programmes, reduction of advertising and increasing the price of tobacco and alcohol. Strong penalties for major drug traffickers must be imposed.

2.12.7.2. The RDP must aim to promote mental health and increase the quality, quantity and accessibility of mental health support and counselling services, particularly for those affected by domestic or other violence, by rape or by child abuse.

2.12.7.3. The RDP must seek to improve community care, rehabilitation and education for all disabled people, particularly the mentally disabled, and must support their families and care-givers. It must also increase access to relaxing environments such as recreational facilities.

2.12.7.4. There are deep divisions, fuelled by mutual suspicion and lack of communication, between traditional and other complementary healers and medical and social workers. This is not in the interests of people who use all types of healers. The RDP must aim to improve communication, understanding and cooperation between different types of healers.

2.12.8. **Sexual health and AIDS.** A programme to combat the spread of sexually transmitted diseases (STDs) and AIDS must include the active and early treatment of these diseases at all health facilities, plus mass education programmes which involve the mass media, schools and community organisations. The treatment of AIDS sufferers and those testing HIV positive must be with utmost respect for their continuing contributions to society. Discrimination will not be tolerated. AIDS education for rural communities, and especially for women, is a priority.

2.12.9. **Other health care programmes.**

2.12.9.1. There must be a programme to ensure the prevention, early detection and treatment of specific priority diseases, including tuberculosis, carcinoma of the cervix, hypertension and diabetes.

2.12.9.2. The RDP must ensure improved access to emergency health services through the provision of more 24-hour emergency services accessible to communities. Access to services must be improved by the development of emergency response centres and appropriate transport and ambulance services, especially in rural areas.

2.12.9.3. There must be a programme to provide appropriate care for chronic diseases and the promotion of healthy lifestyles.

2.12.9.4. A unit within the NHS must coordinate and monitor services aimed at youth, in particular education campaigns to combat substance abuse, teenage parenthood and sexually transmitted diseases amongst the youth.

2.12.9.5. Occupational health services must be greatly expanded and legislation to protect the health of workers must be enforced.

Particular attention must be given to protecting the health of the most vulnerable, including domestic, farm and commercial-sex workers. Workers must have a say in the application of laws, through their health and safety committees. Workers should be given check-ups for major diseases in the workplace. Penalties for violation of occupational health standards must be stricter. Laws must conform to International Labour Organisation standards and other international standards, and unions and state agencies must be empowered to monitor and enforce safety and health standards. An overhaul of workmen's compensation must include administrative restructuring to ensure swifter payment, increasing the coverage for permanently disabled workers to realistic levels, minimum benefit levels in support of low-wage workers, greater use of the compensation system to encourage better workplace health and safety standards, and a combined board to deal with preventive and compensatory aspects of worker safety and health.

2.12.9.6. The appropriate use of technology, especially sophisticated and expensive technology, is very important. A National Advisory Board on health technology should be established and should include representatives from all levels of the NHS. The Advisory Board must develop appropriate and rational policies, devise a system of quality control, and advise on regulations governing the importation and use of expensive technologies.

2.12.9.7. An effective National Health Information System is essential for rational planning and must be introduced. This system must ensure that accurate and comparable data are collected from all parts of the health system, that data are analysed at health-facility, district, provincial and national levels, and that those collecting the data see it as a useful and interesting activity. Mechanisms must be established for sharing information between different programmes and sectors.

2.12.9.8. A programme of Essential National Health Research must be initiated. This should increase consultation with patients, and should help to overcome the isolation and fragmentation of research efforts and to strengthen links between research, policy and action. Special attention must be directed to health systems research in order to improve the effectiveness of health service delivery.

2.12.10. **Human resources for the NHS.**

2.12.10.1. Core teams must be provided for every Community Health Centre and clinic. This will require incentives to attract staff to underserviced (especially rural) areas and increased training of Community Health Workers and Environmental Health Officers.

2.12.10.2. There must be a programme of retraining and reorienting all existing health workers to the Primary Health Care approach. The aim is to train 25 per cent of district health personnel by the end of 1995, and 50 per cent by the end of 1997.

2.12.10.3. Redistribution of personnel will be achieved through more appropriate training, through incentives to work in underserviced areas, through limiting openings for private practice in overserviced areas, and through contractual obligations for those receiving subsidised training.

2.12.10.4. Throughout the period of reconstruction and development strenuous efforts must be made to strengthen the public sector, to attract health workers in private practice back into the public sector, at least on a sessional basis, and to encourage active cooperation between the sectors with the common goal of improving the health of the nation.

2.12.10.5. One of the most important parts of the RDP in the health sector will be the complete transformation of health worker training. This must involve improving human resource planning and management systems; reviewing all training programmes; reviewing selection procedures, and developing new (and often short) training programmes to reorient existing personnel and to train new categories and auxiliary workers.

2.12.10.6. There is a particular need to train existing and new staff in the PHC approach, in management, in primary clinical care, in environmental health, in health promotion and advocacy, in occupational health and in the maintenance and repair of equipment.

2.12.11. **Finance and drugs for the NHS.**

2.12.11.1. The RDP must significantly shift the budget allocation from curative hospital services towards Primary Health Care to address the needs of the majority of the people. This must be done mainly by reallocating staff and budgets to district health services.

2.12.11.2. Within a period of five years a whole range of services must be available free to the aged, the disabled, the unemployed and to students who cannot afford health care.

2.12.11.3. Essential drugs must be provided in all PHC facilities. An essential drugs list must be established to reduce the current wasteful expenditure on inappropriate drugs.

2.12.11.4. The costs of medication in the private sector can be dramatically reduced through greater use of essential drug lists coupled with a single, nationally negotiated and well-publicised price for a given quantity of each drug.

2.13 SOCIAL SECURITY AND SOCIAL WELFARE

2.13.1.   Apartheid contributed to the destruction of family and community life in various ways. The present racially-based, discriminatory social welfare services are piecemeal responses. They have little impact on the root causes of social problems and on the disintegration of the social fabric.

2.13.2.   The RDP aims to transform the existing social welfare policies, programmes and delivery systems so as to ensure basic welfare rights are provided to all South Africans, prioritising those who have been historically disadvantaged.

2.13.3.   **Social welfare as a focus on basic needs and development.** Social welfare includes the right to basic needs such as shelter, food, health care, work opportunities, income security and all those aspects that promote the physical, social and emotional wellbeing of all people in our society, with special provision made for those who are unable to provide for themselves because of specific problems.

2.13.4.   The goals of a developmental social welfare programme are:

2.13.4.1.   the attainment of basic social welfare rights for all South Africans, irrespective of race, colour, religion, gender and physical disability, through the establishment of a democratically-determined, just and effective social delivery system;

2.13.4.2.   the redressing of past imbalances through a deliberate process of affirmative action in respect of those who have been historically disadvantaged, especially women, children, youth, the disabled, people in rural communities and informal settlements;

2.13.4.3.   the empowerment of individuals, families and communities to participate in the process of deciding on the range of needs and problems to be addressed through local, provincial and national initiatives, and

2.13.4.4. the recognition of the role of organs of civil society in the welfare system, such as community-based rehabilitation centres and organisations, non-governmental development organisations, civic associations, the private sector, religious organisations, traditional and other complementary healers, trade unions and individual initiatives, and the establishment of guidelines for mutual cooperation.

2.13.5. A comprehensive, non-racial, unitary and democratic welfare system, including a negotiated national social security programme, must be introduced to aid the distribution of goods and services within the framework of public responsibility.

2.13.6. **The policy and legislative framework.** There must be a comprehensive review of all the policies and legislation regulating social welfare and social security. In particular the National Welfare Act of 1978, the Social Work Act of 1978, and Acts dealing with child and family welfare must be changed. New umbrella legislation which provides the framework for a development-oriented social welfare system based on the principles of equality, equity, access, user involvement and empowerment, and public accountability must be developed.

2.13.7. **The national social welfare delivery system.**

2.13.7.1. The RDP must ensure the greatest coverage in terms of benefits to the poorest through a restructured, integrated social welfare delivery system at national, provincial and local government levels. Unnecessary bureaucratic procedures must be removed.

2.13.7.2. All the key players at local, provincial and national levels responsible for the administration and service-delivery aspects of social welfare must be brought together to find ways of overcoming the difficulties in the present social welfare structure.

2.13.7.3. The restructuring of the social welfare system and services at national, provincial, district and local community levels must be in line with international norms and standards.

2.13.7.4. The planning, coordination and evaluation of social services must take place with community and inter-sectoral involvement.

2.13.8. **A national Social Welfare and Development Department.**

2.13.8.1. The national department must be responsible for the development of national policies, standards and norms, setting of priorities and targets, drawing up of the national budget on social welfare and allocating resources and grants to targeted areas.

2.13.8.2. The development of service conditions and professional standards to guide the training, education and employment of social service personnel must be the responsibility of the national department.

2.13.8.3. The national department must be responsible for the monitoring and evaluation of the implementation of social welfare goals and priorities.

2.13.9. **Provincial social welfare and development departments.**

2.13.9.1. Each province must have a social welfare and development department. Such departments must be responsible for the planning, coordination, regulation, provision and evaluation of social welfare and community development services required at provincial and district levels.

2.13.9.2. Provincial departments must be responsible for social services at preventive (primary) and curative (secondary) levels. The management and distribution of social services at provincial, district and community levels must fall within the provincial department's authority.

2.13.10. **Social security.** The national social security system must be designed to meet the needs of workers in both formal and informal sectors, and of the unemployed, through:

2.13.10.1. social insurance which includes compulsory private contributory pension schemes or provident funds for all workers, and state social pensions;

2.13.10.2. linking contributory pension/provident funds and non-contributory schemes, as well as the transfer of contributory pensions, and

2.13.10.3. criteria which entitle workers to retire between the ages of 60 and 65, or to a social pension at 60.

2.13.11. **Social safety net.** Social assistance in the form of cash or in-kind benefits should be given to those most at risk (such social assistance could take the form of work opportunities in public works programmes; the provision of food, clothing and health care to those in need; cash in the form of disability grants, foster care grants, maintenance grants, or grants for veterans according to predetermined criteria).

2.13.12. The RDP aims to establish a national coordinating body with representation of workers, community members, the social welfare sector, the private sector, government and other appropriate organisations to review existing legislation, policies and procedures and to monitor the implementation of a transformed social security system.

2.13.13. Social security measures must initially focus on the needs of those who have been historically disadvantaged, such as domestic workers, agricultural workers, seasonal workers, workers who are disabled, women, the homeless, and families in rural and informal settlements.

2.13.14. Social welfare rights and the distribution of benefits must be guided by the principles of user empowerment and participation through community- and worker-based citizens-rights education programmes.

2.13.15. The RDP must focus on the reconstruction of family and community life by prioritising and responding to the needs of families with no income, women and children who have been victims of domestic and other forms of violence, young offenders and all those affected by substance abuse.

2.13.16. A comprehensive range of social service programmes must be developed in partnership with community-based structures to respond to the specific needs of the elderly and those in chronic emotional distress. Community-based and community-planned rehabilitation programmes must be encouraged to meet the needs of the disabled, and the democratic government must make adequate resources available for rehabilitation.

2.13.17. **Children.** The rights of children must be protected and measures must be taken to ensure that community-based and workplace care centres are provided for children in need of alternate care. The RDP must ensure that immediate steps are taken to remove all children from prisons and police cells. Alternate detention centres with proper health facilities, counselling and other support services must be provided for children. Special programmes protecting homeless children, especially those on the streets, must be put into place.

2.13.18. **Human resources for the Social Welfare and Development Department.** The existing pool of social service workers and their conditions of service must be reviewed. The present number of social workers (approximately 7 500) is inadequate, and their training is often inappropriate. Many social workers must be reoriented and retrained within a developmental approach to social welfare. The national, provincial and local social welfare departments must have both specialised and generic social service personnel at management, middle-management and operational levels. The curricula of social welfare and community development educational institutions must be reviewed. Within a five-year period a minimum of another 3 000 community development workers must be trained to work within provincial and local government structures to aid the process of prioritisation of community needs and allocation of resources. Social service managers must be trained with due regard to the need for affirmative action.

2.13.19. **Inter-sectoral coordination.** Inter-sectoral units on areas such as mental health, child care, women, and juvenile justice must be developed to plan and implement integrated strategies aimed at improving services to these target groups. In addition, the relationship between social welfare, health, community development and labour institutions and related sectors must be improved.

3.
Developing Our Human Resources

3.1 PROBLEM STATEMENT

3.1.1. Education and training under apartheid is characterised by three key features. First, the system is fragmented along racial and ethnic lines, and is saturated with the racist and sexist ideology and educational doctrines of apartheid. Second, there is a lack of access or unequal access to education and training at all levels of the system. Vast disparities exist between black and white provision, and large numbers of people – in particular, adults (and more especially women), out-of-school youth, and children of pre-school age – have little or no access to education and training. Third, there is a lack of democratic control within the education and training system. Students, teachers, parents and workers are excluded from decision-making processes.

3.1.2. The fragmented, unequal and undemocratic nature of the education and training system has profound effects on the development of the economy and society. It results in the destruction, distortion or neglect of the human potential of our country, with devastating consequences for social and economic development. This is evident in the lack of career paths offered to workers and in the effect this has on worker motivation and the general productivity of the economy. And more importantly, apartheid education and its aftermath of resistance destroyed the culture of learning in large sections of our communities, leading, in the worst-affected areas, to a virtual breakdown of schooling and conditions of anarchy in relations between students, teachers, principals, and the education authorities.

3.1.3. Under colonialism and apartheid, the culture of the majority of the population was suppressed. People and communities were denied resources and facilities to develop their own cultural expression. High illiteracy rates, the lack of an effective educational system, and extreme poverty compounded this cultural deprivation. The state, special interest groups and wealthy South Africans promoted distorted culture in order to accommodate apartheid ideology and needs, with a bias toward Eurocentric high art.

3.1.4.   Women and the youth bear the brunt of these injustices, with the consequence that special attention must be given to these sectors of society in the planning and implementation of human resources development policies and strategies. Many of the youth are presently outside the socio-economic mainstream of the country.

3.1.5.   The challenge that we face at the dawning of a democratic society is to create an education and training system that ensures people are able to realise their full potential in our society, as a basis and a prerequisite for the successful achievement of all other goals in this Reconstruction and Development Programme.

3.2   VISION AND OBJECTIVES

3.2.1.   Human resources, unlike other resources, think for themselves! People are, and must remain, the architects of the RDP as it unfolds in the years to come. The provision of opportunities for people to develop themselves in order to improve the quality of their own lives and the standard of living of their communities is a central objective of the RDP, alongside ensuring that basic needs are met, the society is democratised and the economy grows.

3.2.2.   The opportunities that must be provided include a massive expansion and qualitative improvement in the education and training system, artistic and cultural expression, and sport and recreation.

3.2.3.   Human resource development must address the development of human capabilities, abilities, knowledge and knowhow to meet the people's ever-growing needs for goods and services, to improve their standard of living and quality of life. It is a process in which the citizens of a nation acquire and develop the knowledge and skill necessary for occupational tasks and for other social, cultural, intellectual, and political roles that are part and parcel of a vibrant democratic society.

3.3 EDUCATION AND TRAINING

3.3.1. We must develop an integrated system of education and training that provides equal opportunities to all irrespective of race, colour, sex, class, language, age, religion, geographical location, political or other opinion. It must address the development of knowledge and skills that can be used to produce high-quality goods and services in such a way as to enable us to develop our cultures, our society and our economy.

3.3.2. Education must be directed to the full development of the individual and community, and to strengthening respect for human rights and fundamental freedoms. It must promote understanding, tolerance, and friendship among all South Africans and must advance the principles contained in the Bill of Rights.

3.3.3. A new national human resources development strategy must be based on the principles of democracy, non-racism, non-sexism, equity and redress to avoid the pitfalls of the past.

3.3.4. The democratic government has the ultimate responsibility for ensuring that our human resources are developed to the full. Education, training and development opportunities must be provided in accordance with national standards. However, civil society must be encouraged to play an active part in the provision of learning opportunities as part of the national human resources development strategy. For example, democratic school governance structures must be set up which involve democratically elected parent and teacher representatives, as well as providing for student participation at a consultative level.

3.3.5. **Mechanisms, institutions and legislation.** Success in rebuilding and expanding education and training depends on having an effective and responsive organisation to manage change. The education and training bureaucracy must be reorganised at national, sectoral and provincial levels through the establishment of:

3.3.5.1.   a single national ministry responsible for education and training, to set national policies, norms and standards throughout the system, to undertake planning and provide budgetary resources for all aspects of education and training, and to manage higher education and training development;

3.3.5.2.   provincial departments responsible for education and training, to plan and manage all aspects of education and training provision other than higher education;

3.3.5.3.   statutory bodies, based on appropriate democratic representation of stakeholders, to establish standards and advise the national ministry and provincial departments on policy and development programmes in education and training;

3.3.5.4.   industry-based education and training boards with union and employer participation, to design and implement programmes within industries (with such boards partly financed by industry), consisten with the standards developed for the integrated national framework;

3.3.5.5.   structures of institutional governance which reflect the interests of all stakeholders and the broader community served by the institution, and

3.3.5.6.   a statutory South African Qualifications Authority with responsibility for accreditation, certification and the maintenance of national standards.

3.3.6.   **Girls and women in education and training.** Girls and women are frequently denied education and training opportunities because they are female.

Furthermore, girls and women are educated and trained to fulfil traditional roles which perpetuate their oppression. Within all education and training programmes special attention must be given to the special interests of girls and women. For example, adult basic education and training programmes should give special emphasis to women trapped in the rural areas. Campaigns and information should also open up a wider range of learning opportunities and choices for women, which in turn should lead to a wider range of income-generating forms of employment. Girls and women should be encouraged to pursue non-traditional subjects such as maths and science, for example. However, in addition to these measures, special steps must be taken to give full recognition and value to the work and skills that are traditionally associated with women. Where appropriate these should be recognised within the national qualifications framework.

3.3.7. **An integrated qualifications framework.** By establishing a national qualifications framework which integrates all elements of the education and training system, we must enable learners to progress to higher levels from any starting point. They must be able to obtain recognition and credits for qualifications and credits towards qualifications from one part of the system to another. The system must enable assessment and recognition of prior learning and skills acquired through experience. To this end, curricula should cut across traditional divisions of skills and knowledge.

3.3.8. **Early childhood educare.** Educare, which introduces an educational component into child care, must be an integral part of a future education and training system. The provision of educare for young children is an important step toward lifetime learning and the emancipation of women. We must expand early childhood educare by supporting an increase in private and public funding; institutionalising it within the ministry and the provincial departments, and raising national awareness of the importance of such programmes. The democratic government also bears the ultimate responsibility for training, upgrading and setting national standards for educare providers, with the assistance of civil society.

3.3.9.   **Adult basic education and training.**

3.3.9.1.   Adult Basic Education (ABE) aims to provide adults with education and training programmes equivalent to exit level in the formal school system, with an emphasis on literacy and numeracy skills. This represents a crucial step in the reconstruction and development of our society. Special provision must be made for ABE within the future national ministry and government departments at all levels. ABE must conform to standards set out within the national qualifications.

3.3.9.2.   The provision of ABE must be expanded by building a partnership of all employer, labour, local and provincial government, community and funding agencies. This will establish a process to provide funding support to a national ABE programme, managed at provincial, sectoral, local, community and workplace levels, and where possible using existing educational and training facilities when these are unutilised or underutilised, such as at night, over weekends and during holidays.

3.3.9.3.   ABE must be centrally included in all reconstruction projects, and particularly programmes for the unemployed. Micro enterprises must also be given assistance with respect to ABE. Such provision should assist learners to seek related employment on completion of the specific project.

3.3.10.   **Special education.** Under minority rule and apartheid, the learning needs of children and adults with physical or other disabilities and impairments suffered massive neglect. The RDP must redress this situation by establishing appropriate institutional structures and inter-sectoral groups, mounting a national advocacy campaign to raise awareness of the issue, ensuring that existing facilities are optimally used, and developing new programmes as needed. The education and training needs of the disabled and other marginalised groups should be catered for as part of a process of facilitating access to facilities and to the economy, so that disadvantaged groups are seen as an asset – by themselves and by society at large.

3.3.11. **Compulsory school education.**

3.3.11.1. The democratic government must restructure the education and training systems to meet the needs of all. We must foster community participation and a culture of teaching and learning. We must develop a national qualifications system that should recognise learners' skills, experience and studies, allowing them to gain access to different kinds of education and training throughout their lives, and letting people re-enter education and training easily.

3.3.11.2. The democratic government must enable all children to go to school for at least 10 years. The 10-year compulsory general education cycle should proceed from a pre-school reception year to the present Standard 7. The government must phase in compulsory education as soon as possible. To achieve this objective we must rebuild and expand our schools. Classes of 50-80 or more students are unacceptable. We must ensure that no class exceeds 40 students by the end of the decade.

3.3.11.3. In addition, we must align the structure, curricula and certification with the new national qualifications system.

3.3.11.4. Education from the present Standard 8 up to the present Standard 10 must be redesigned and incorporated into an integrated post-compulsory phase of learning, coordinated at national level and resulting in a Further Education Certificate (or National Higher Certificate). This will integrate post-compulsory schooling with training and should replace the matric with a Further

Education Certificate or National Higher Certificate.

3.3.11.5. The new programmes, curricula and teaching approaches for the first four years of school must take into account the language, learning and developmental needs of young children.

3.3.11.6. The need for school buildings must be addressed by vastly improved use of existing facilities and a school-building programme. To this end all schools and existing facilities are to be used to full capacity by the start of 1995 for both compulsory and non-compulsory learning, and schools must be built in sufficient numbers to meet the real demand. We must empower school communities to take responsibility for the care and protection of their schools.

3.3.11.7. Farm schools and community schools must be progressively integrated into the ordinary school system, and additional schools must be provided in commercial farming areas.

3.3.11.8. The existing curriculum bears the mark of racism, sexism, authoritarianism and outmoded teaching practices. Transformation is essential. Curriculum change takes time, but we must find points of entry to permit reconstruction to start in 1994. Major stakeholders must reach agreement through the National Education and Training Forum on the management of curriculum and examinations in the transition period. We must establish institutes for curriculum development at national and provincial levels.

3.3.11.9. Black education, in particular, suffered severe deficits in the areas of science, mathematics, technology, arts and culture. Curriculum development must therefore pay special attention to these areas.

3.3.12. **Further education and training.**

3.3.12.1. Further education and training is the term used in this document to refer to those education and training experiences which follow compulsory general education or its equivalent and culminate in the National Higher Certificate.

3.3.12.2. Further education must provide schooling, training and adult education as an integrated system. A balanced and flexible curriculum leading to the National Higher Certificate must be developed for all learners in a variety of learning contexts: students learning within formal institutions, workers in industry, out-of-school youth, and adults learning in community learning centres. The curriculum must seek to open learning paths consistent with the goals of lifelong learning.

3.3.13. **Higher education.**

3.3.13.1. The higher education system represents a major resource for national development and contributes to the world-wide advance of knowledge. But its present structure and capacity are seriously distorted by the apartheid inheritance, its governance systems are outmoded, and its funding arrangements have led to serious crises for both the students and the institutions themselves.

3.3.13.2. In order to address these structural problems with the seriousness they deserve, the new democratic government will consult all significant stakeholders with a view to appointing a representative and expert higher education commission to investigate and report urgently on the role of the higher education sector in national reconstruction and development; the structure of the system; access/selection and exclusion; the role of open learning and distance education; institutional governance and the governance of the system as a whole;

capacity-building and affirmative action in academic and administrative appointments; the resource base for higher education, and the system of student finance.

3.3.14. **Teachers, educators and trainers.**

3.3.14.1. The reconstruction of education and training requires a body of teachers, educators and trainers committed to RDP goals and competent in carrying them out. This requires that they are able to understand and respond flexibly to the challenges of the new approaches to curriculum, method, delivery and certification which an integrated system of education and training demands. They must dedicate themselves to enhancing the quality of learning and achievement throughout the system. Teachers, educators and trainers who are inadequately educated, badly treated by their employers, and poorly rewarded cannot be expected to fulfil these expectations.

3.3.14.2. For adult basic education and training, the problems faced are those of insufficient and poor-quality training opportunities for facilitators, non-existent qualifications and career paths, and very low status. For school teachers, problems range from poor initial training, to insufficient support services and low wages and poor conditions. The reconstruction of education and training requires an overhaul of teacher/educator/trainer training and the industrial relations system in line with other sectors.

3.3.14.3. Statutory national and provincial teacher, educator and trainer development centres should be established to review all relevant education and training curriculum and support services. They must take special measures to increase the supply and competence of maths, science and art teachers for schools, and educators/trainers for the non-compulsory learning sectors.

3.3.14.4. A transparent, participatory and equitable process to review salaries and conditions of service will be established. It will guarantee a living wage to the worst-paid teachers. It will also establish appropriate career paths, introduce criteria for the recognition and grading of teachers and trainers, and promote professional development within the proposed national qualifications framework.

3.3.15. **Restructuring training within an integrated education and training system.**

3.3.15.1. The RDP proposes a substantially restructured and expanded training system, integrated with Adult Basic Education, post-Standard 7 formal schooling and higher education.

3.3.15.2. The national qualifications framework must be the mechanism by means of which this integration is given effect.

3.3.15.3. The national ministry and provincial departments of education and training must consult with the restructured bodies of civil society on policy issues.

3.3.15.4. Education and training for skills development must be modular and outcome-based; must recognise prior learning and experience; must develop transferable and portable skills; must have common standards, and must be integrated within the national qualifications and accreditation system. Training programmes and schooling after Standard 7 should form part of an integrated system. Training for self-employment is essential and must be offered.

3.4 ARTS AND CULTURE

3.4.1.   Arts and culture embrace custom, tradition, belief, religion, language, crafts, and all the artforms like music, dance, the visual arts, film, theatre, written and oral literature. Arts and culture permeate all aspects of society and are integral parts of social and economic life, as well as business and industry based upon the arts.

3.4.2.   Under colonialism and apartheid the culture of the majority of South Africans was neglected, distorted and suppressed. Freedom of expression and creativity were stifled. People and communities were denied access to resources and facilities to exercise and develop their need for cultural and artistic expression. Illiteracy, the lack of an effective educational system, and extreme poverty compounded this cultural deprivation.

3.4.3.   The RDP arts and culture policies aim to:

3.4.3.1.   affirm and promote the rich and diverse expression of South African culture – all people must be guaranteed the right to practise their culture, language, beliefs and customs, as well as enjoy freedom of expression and creativity free from interference;

3.4.3.2.   promote the development of a unifying national culture, representing the aspirations of all South Africa's people (this cannot be imposed, but requires educating people in principles of non-racialism, non-sexism, human rights and democracy);

3.4.3.3.   ensure that resources and facilities for both the production and the appreciation of arts and culture are made available and accessible to all (priority must be given to those people and communities previously denied access to these resources);

3.4.3.4.   conserve, promote and revitalise our national cultural heritage so it is accessible to all communities (historical and cultural collections, resources and sites must fully reflect the many components of our cultural heritage and, in particular, neglected and suppressed aspects of our people's culture must be conserved);

3.4.3.5. place arts education firmly within the national educational curricula, as well as in non-formal educational structures;

3.4.3.6. link culture firmly to areas of national priority such as health, housing, tourism, etc., to ensure that culture is entrenched as a fundamental component of development;

3.4.3.7. establish and implement a language policy that encourages and supports, financially and otherwise, the utilisation of all the languages of South Africa, and

3.4.3.8. cooperate with educational bodies and the media in eradicating illiteracy, and in promoting a reading and learning culture.

3.4.4. A Ministry of Arts and Culture must be established to implement these objectives.

3.4.5. Existing publicly funded and parastatal cultural and arts structures, such as the Performing Arts Councils, the National Gallery, museums, libraries, archives and monuments, must be democratised. Commissions to investigate the organisation, funding, policies and future roles of such structures must be established as a matter of urgency. These commissions should report within six months of their appointment, and complete the tasks of transformation within two years.

3.4.6. Ultimately government is responsible for the provision of cultural amenities for each community. As an immediate measure, established community art centres should be subsidised by government. In the longer term, the Ministry of Arts and Culture should work with local and regional government and community structures to form community art centres throughout the country.

3.4.7. With local and provincial government, the Ministry should establish libraries, museums, galleries, monuments and historical sites. These should reflect the many different strands of South African culture. Each community should have these facilities located within reach.

3.4.8. Arts education should be an integral part of the national school curricula at primary, secondary and tertiary level, as well as in non-formal education. Urgent attention must be given to the creation of relevant arts curricula, teacher training, and provision of facilities for the arts within all schools.

3.4.9. Nationally and within each region, democratic Arts Councils will be established as statutory bodies. Allocations to such bodies will be made by the government, operating within its policy framework. Principles along which government funding will be disbursed must include redressing imbalances of the past, transformation and development, non-racialism, non-sexism, human rights and democracy.

3.4.10. The Pan-South African Language Institute proposed in the Interim Constitution must be constituted as a matter of urgency, to devise programmes and seek resources to develop all South African languages and particularly the historically neglected indigenous languages.

3.4.11. The government will encourage and facilitate cultural exchange between the people of South Africa and the rest of the world. This exchange will be informed by the views of cultural workers and associations and will be aimed at promoting local developmental programmes and international understanding.

3.4.12. A statutory national body should be created to encourage the development of a healthy, vibrant and diverse local South African film and audio-visual industry, reflecting the realities of all the people of South Africa. This body should work to give the majority of South African viewers and audio-visual practitioners access to audio-visual communications.

3.4.13. Legislation hindering the development of the arts (for example, censorship laws) must be repealed. Legislation should be adopted based on principles of transformation, reconstruction and development, and in line with international conventions on the arts, labour legislation protecting cultural workers, and copyright laws.

3.4.14. We must develop human resources to fulfil these objectives, in part through employing additional civil servants on a contract or permanent basis, as well as through retraining existing personnel.

3.4.15. The Ministry of Arts and Culture must have its own budget. Funding for arts and culture will also be obtained through encouraging partnerships between government, business, non-governmental organisations, communities, and the international community. Within this framework, the national budget will carry an allocation specifically for culture. The framework will make provision for tax incentives and rebates to encourage investment in arts and culture.

3.5 SPORT AND RECREATION

3.5.1. One of the cruellest legacies of apartheid is its distortion of sport and recreation in our society, the enforced segregation of these activities and the gross neglect in providing facilities for the majority of South Africa's people. This has denied millions of people and particularly our youth the right to a normal and healthy life.

3.5.2. It is important to ensure that sporting and recreational facilities are available to all South African communities. Participation in sporting and recreational activities should reflect the country's demographics. The removal of obstacles that preclude specific sections of the community from participation is crucial. This cannot be left entirely in the hands of individual sporting codes or local communities, both of whom require support and encouragement.

3.5.3. Sport and recreation are an integral part of reconstructing and developing a healthier society. Sport and recreation should cut across all developmental programmes, and be accessible and affordable for all

South Africans, including those in rural areas, the young and the elderly. The RDP must facilitate the mobilising of resources in both the public and private sectors to redress inequalities and enhance this vital aspect of our society.

3.5.4.   Particular attention must be paid to the provision of facilities at schools and in communities where there are large concentrations of unemployed youth. Sport and recreation are an integral and important part of education and youth programmes. In developing such programmes it should be recognised that sport is played at different levels of competence and that there are different specific needs at different levels.

3.5.5.   The new democratic government must work with the National Sports Commission in developing and implementing a sports policy. This should include issues such as the establishment of an independent national sports controlling agency for the control of drugs in sport, as well as a national sports academy to undertake and coordinate training programmes concerning coaching, refereeing, umpiring and sports management.

3.6   YOUTH DEVELOPMENT

3.6.1.   The high levels of youth unemployment require special programmes. A national youth service programme is already giving young people structured work experience while continuing their education and training. The programme should not just be seen as a job creation measure, however, but as youth development and capacity building. Care must be taken to ensure that the programme does not displace or substitute workers in permanent employment.

3.6.2.   Youth development more generally must focus on education and training, job creation, and enabling young people to realise their full potential and participate fully in the society and their future. It must restore the hope of our youth in the future, and in their capacity to channel their resourcefulness and energy into reconstruction and development.

3.6.3.   The national youth service programme must better educate, develop, train and empower youth, and enable them to participate in the reconstruction of society through involvement in service projects in the community such as literacy, welfare, and improving infrastructure. All development and job creation programmes such as a national public works programme must address the problem of youth alienation and unemployment.

3.6.4.   A national institution must coordinate the programme in consultation with other sectors. Areas in which the youth service programme could contribute include educare and literacy programmes, health, environmental protection, rural and urban infrastructure development, and peace monitoring. The programme must also be used to enhance awareness of the relationships between productivity, the economy and the role of science and technology in achieving the objectives of the RDP. Finally, the youth service programme must also build a spirit of national unity and reconciliation amongst the youth, as well as a sense of service towards the community and the nation.

3.6.5.   Appropriate government departments must more forcefully represent youth interests, including through the allocation of resources to organisations involved in youth work. An autonomous National Youth Council should be given support in coordinating youth activities, lobbying for the rights of young people, and representing South Africa internationally. A review of legislation affecting youth and the implementation of youth service programmes must also be carried out.

3.6.6.   The democratic government must support the International Convention on the Rights of the Child, and the supporting Plan of Action. It must work to protect the lives of children, to promote the full development of their human potential, and to make them aware of their needs, rights and opportunities. The needs of children must be paramount throughout all programmes aimed at meeting basic needs and socio-economic upliftment.

4.
Building the Economy

4.1 PROBLEM STATEMENT

4.1.1.   The South African economy is in a deep-seated structural crisis and as such requires fundamental reconstruction. For decades forces within the white minority have used their exclusive access to political and economic power to promote their own sectional interests at the expense of black people. Black people have been systematically exploited and oppressed economically and South Africa now has one of the world's most unequal patterns of distribution of income and wealth. A disproportionate share of the burden of poverty and inequality has fallen on black women who have been subject to systematic gender oppression. Economic deprivation has created a fertile base for the violence and instability now engulfing our country. The ever-changing and destabilising global economy has also adversely affected the local economy.

4.1.2.   Marked regional disparities exist within the economy as a result of policies designed to ensure a migratory labour supply to the mines and of the ethnic division of South Africa under the apartheid system. Enforced segregation and industrial decentralisation have located whole communities in areas where their economic viability is threatened. A few metropolitan regions account for the bulk of national production, while some provinces are affected by a crisis of unemployment, and can barely afford to provide basic services. Almost half the black population was compelled to live in so-called 'homelands' where per capita incomes are less than a quarter of the national average.

4.1.3.   Successive minority governments and business have tried to promote growth by encouraging local production of manufactured goods which were previously imported. This policy led to the emergence of a significant manufacturing sector in our country.

However, the disparity between the low income levels of the majority of consumers and factors leading to rising price levels ensured that the manufacturing sector served the wealthy and excluded the poor. The sector is in general characterised by poor productivity and an undue dependence upon low wages. It makes little contribution to foreign exchange earnings, but depends to a very great extent on imported machinery and equipment paid for out of foreign exchange earned by mineral exports.

4.1.4.   Over the past decade and more, growth stagnated, investment dropped precipitously and average real incomes declined. The economy remains dependent on mineral exports, and the manufacturing sector cannot create jobs, meet the basic needs of the majority or compete on world markets. The decline in investment within the public and private sectors, and capital flight, have contributed to an ageing capital stock and contraction in the manufacturing sector. Capacity utilisation of manufacturing plant and equipment remains at very low levels. Speculative investment has replaced productive investment, with a consequent decline in job creation and overall employment levels.

4.1.5.   The South African economy is also characterised by excessive concentration of economic power in the hands of a tiny minority of the population. Through the pyramid system and the resultant control over a vast network of subsidiary companies, a small number of very large conglomerates now dominate the production, distribution and financial sectors. In addition there is a high degree of monopolisation and blatant anti-competitive tendencies such as predatory pricing and interlocking directorships in certain industries. With regard to land, white ownership and often corporate ownership are overwhelming. Not only does this create racial and social tension, but it is to be seriously doubted that such high levels of concentration can be economically beneficial.

4.1.6.   A particular weakness of the economy, aggravated by racist and sexist policies, is the inability to maintain a dynamic small-scale and micro enterprise sector. Smaller firms, especially if owned by black people, can rarely develop productive linkages with the large-scale sector.

Most people in the informal sector lack productive and managerial skills plus access to business sites, capital and markets. They face an array of repressive regulations originally designed to undermine black business and farming.

4.1.7.   A critical cause of inefficiency and inequality lies in the position of labour. Economic growth depended on the centrality of the cheap labour system. Rigid hierarchies and oppressive labour relations ignored the skills latent in our experienced industrial workforce. Apartheid laws denied workers their basic rights. High levels of unemployment and oppressive legislation made it difficult even for organised workers to maintain a living wage. The lack of skills forms a major obstacle to the development of a modern economy able to support a decent living standard for all our people. The apartheid state also systematically excluded workers from collective bargaining and policy-making at national and shop-floor levels. While the struggles of organised workers have reversed this to some extent, the right to strike continues to be limited, farm and domestic workers do not have basic rights, the majority of workers earn low wages, and there are enormous wage differentials.

4.1.8.   Only a quarter as many women as men hold jobs in the formal sector. High unemployment, the migrant labour system and the difficulties facing the informal sector hit women particularly hard. Within formal employment, women are discriminated against in many areas such as wages, job security, specific needs of women workers, and employment opportunities. The migrant labour system continues to disempower both workers and their families.

4.1.9.   The agricultural sector and rural economy are also in crisis. Many white-owned farms are deeply indebted and vast tracts of land designated for occupation by whites are inefficiently cultivated. Many thousands of black rural households are, meanwhile, crammed into tiny plots unable to produce or buy affordable food. Government decentralisation policies have failed to channel resources to the rural areas which remain the most deprived parts of the country.

4.1.10.   The apartheid state's economic agencies have been contradictory and secretive, and were subordinate to apartheid's logic and the siege-economy mentality. Parastatals such as the Industrial Development Corporation (IDC), Development Bank of Southern Africa (DBSA) and the Small Business Development Corporation (SBDC) could be immensely important in driving industrial, socio-economic and infrastructural development. But in recent years, under the cloak of secrecy, the apartheid state privatised or commercialised many agencies in the public sector (such as Transnet, Eskom, Telkom, Iscor, Foskor, SAA, the Post Office, Forestry and others). Often this policy, unilaterally imposed for ideological reasons, harmed basic services to the poor or reduced the ability of the state to mobilise resources for development.

4.1.11.   The consequences of such undemocratic state policies in a structurally unbalanced economy include a serious fiscal crisis, with high personal tax rates accompanying a large budget deficit. In addition, the country's balance of payments problems, exacerbated by capital flight, have made it difficult to service the foreign debt incurred during the apartheid era. The need to maintain tight controls over economic policy as a result, has had a devastating effect on economic growth and employment.

4.1.12.   In past years, South Africa's relations with its Southern African neighbours were hostile, and apartheid destabilisation destroyed much of their economic base. Within the South African Customs Union (SACU) there has been no consideration of the differing needs of the participating countries and no common developmental policies.

4.2   VISION AND OBJECTIVES

4.2.1.   The fundamental principles of our economic policy are democracy, participation and development. We are convinced that neither a commandist central planning system nor an unfettered free market system can provide adequate solutions to the problems confronting us. Reconstruction and development will be achieved through the leading and enabling role of the state, a thriving private sector, and active involvement by all sectors of civil society which in combination will lead to sustainable growth.

4.2.2.   Our central goal for reconstruction and development is to create a strong, dynamic and balanced economy which will:

4.2.2.1.   eliminate the poverty, low wages and extreme inequalities in wages and wealth generated by the apartheid system, meet basic needs, and thus ensure that every South African has a decent living standard and economic security;

4.2.2.2.   address economic imbalances and structural problems in industry, trade, commerce, mining, agriculture, finance and labour markets;

4.2.2.3.   address economic imbalances and uneven development within and between South Africa's regions;

4.2.2.4.   ensure that no one suffers discrimination in hiring, promotion or training on the basis of race or gender;

4.2.2.5.   develop the human resource capacity of all South Africans so the economy achieves high skills and wages;

4.2.2.6.   democratise the economy and empower the historically oppressed, particularly the workers and women and their organisations, by encouraging broader participation in decisions about the economy in both the private and public sectors;

4.2.2.7.   create productive employment opportunities at a living wage for all South Africans;

4.2.2.8.   develop a prosperous and balanced regional economy in Southern Africa based on the principles of equity and mutual benefit, and

4.2.2.9.   integrate into the world economy in a manner that sustains a viable and efficient domestic manufacturing capacity and increases our potential to export manufactured products.

It is only by addressing the above that our economy will be capable of sustained growth.

4.2.3.   To carry out programmes to meet these objectives, as well as those outlined in previous chapters, the democratic government must play a leading and enabling role in guiding the economy and the market toward reconstruction and development. Legislative and institutional reform will be effected to enable the implementation of the RDP. We aim to achieve a dynamic balance between government intervention, the private sector and the participation of civil society.

4.2.4.   There must be a significant role for public sector investment to complement the role of the private sector and community participation in stimulating reconstruction and development. The primary question in this regard is not the legal form that government involvement in economic activity might take at any point, but whether such actions must strengthen the ability of the economy to respond to the massive inequalities in the country, relieve the material hardship of the majority of the people, and stimulate economic growth and competitiveness.

4.2.5.   In restructuring the public sector to carry out national goals, the balance of evidence will guide the decision for or against various economic policy measures. The democratic government must therefore consider:

4.2.5.1.   increasing the public sector in strategic areas through, for example, nationalisation, purchasing a shareholding in companies, establishing new public corporations or joint ventures with the private sector, and

4.2.5.2.   reducing the public sector in certain areas in ways that enhance efficiency, advance affirmative action and empower the historically disadvantaged, while ensuring

the protection of both consumers and the
rights and employment of workers.

4.2.6. The RDP will foster a new and constructive relationship
between the people, their organisations in civil society,
key constituencies such as the trade unions and
organised business, the democratic government, and
the workings of the market.

4.2.7. We can only achieve our economic objectives if we
establish transparent, participatory and accountable
policy-making procedures in both the public and private
sectors. The democratic government, the trade union
movement, business associations and the relevant
organisations of civil society must cooperate in
formulating economic policy. The democratic
government must review the inherited economic
departments and agencies to streamline policy-making
and implementation and to define appropriate
relationships with forums and the various tiers of
government.

4.2.8. Economic growth is critical for sustainable
improvements in services and incomes. We must shape
the expansion of the social and economic infrastructure
to stimulate industry and agriculture. These policies
must be coordinated with the development, on a
cooperative basis, of the Southern African region as a
whole. On this foundation, we must establish a dynamic,
integrated economy able to provide higher incomes,
reduce excessive dependence on imports and compete
on foreign markets.

4.2.9. All of our policies must aim to alleviate inequalities in
incomes and wealth and expand productive
opportunities. Critical programmes in this area include
urban and rural development, industrial strategy,
support for small and micro enterprise (including small-
scale farming), job creation, land reform and other
programmes discussed in earlier chapters. The
democratic government must also create laws and
institutions to end discrimination in hiring, promotion
and training.

4.2.10. Our economic policies require human resource
development on a massive scale. Improved training and

education are fundamental to higher employment, the introduction of more advanced technologies, and reduced inequalities. Higher labour productivity will be the result of new attitudes towards work in the context of overall economic reconstruction and development.

4.2.11. Basic to the consultative and interactive approach to economic policy is the protection of worker rights, labour standards and proactive labour market policies. The RDP makes a decisive break with the exploitative cheap-labour policies of apartheid and moves toward education, training, skills, a living wage, and collective bargaining as the basis for enhanced productivity in the economy.

4.3 INTEGRATING RECONSTRUCTION AND DEVELOPMENT

4.3.1. One of the basic principles outlined in Chapter One was that of linking reconstruction and development. This is in contrast to the argument that growth is needed before development is possible, an approach which would leave intact the severe regional, racial and gender and structural imbalances that characterise the present economy. To prevent this from happening, reconstruction and development must be an integrated process. Such integration must be basic to all economic policy. This is where the public sector must play a major enabling role, since it cannot be expected that the market will make such a structural transformation on its own. Yet without such a transformation democracy will not survive, because socio-economic stability will not be achieved.

4.3.2. The RDP's principles recognise the mutually reinforcing nature of urban and rural development strategies through, for example, the benefits of improved agriculture to the urban economy. Strategies for urban and rural development must be integrated within the RDP to ensure that the needs of all our people are met in a balanced and equitable manner. An integrated strategy is essential for the process of unifying our economy and linking reconstruction and development.

4.3.3.   In general, the RDP recognises the need to break down apartheid geography through land reform, more compact cities, decent public transport, and the development of industries and services that use local resources and/or meet local needs. In this context, the RDP must seek to help people generate economic wealth in their chosen communities.

4.3.4.   Macro-economic policies must take into consideration their effect upon the geographic distribution of economic activity. Additional strategies must address the excessive growth of the largest urban centres, the skewed distribution of population within rural areas, the role of small and medium-sized towns, and the future of declining towns and regions, and the apartheid dumping grounds.

4.3.5.   In order to foster the growth of local economies, broadly representative institutions must be established to address local economic development needs. Their purpose would be to formulate strategies to address job creation and community development (for example, leveraging private sector funds for community development, investment strategies, training, small business and agricultural development, etc.). If necessary, the democratic government must provide some subsidies as a catalyst for job creation programmes controlled by communities and/or workers, and target appropriate job creation and development programmes in the most neglected and impoverished areas of our country. Ultimately, all such projects should sustain themselves.

4.3.6.   The incentives for decentralisation introduced under apartheid frequently proved excessively discretionary and open to misuse. Still, in many areas simply eliminating them would cause severe job losses. For this reason, the democratic government must establish clear-cut guidelines and procedures for reviewing decentralisation incentives. Where communities and workers can certify that the subsidies are being utilised in a sustainable, non-exploitative manner, the democratic government must maintain the incentives. Otherwise, it must redirect subsidies to ventures that promote linkages within the local economy.

4.3.7.   The Interim Constitution will have a significant impact on economic growth. Setting up new provinces will affect investment flows, regional assets and fiscal transfers as well as the institutions that make and implement policies. Every province must develop a programme for regional reconstruction and development in the context of the national RDP.

4.3.8.   **Rural development.** The RDP aims to improve the quality of rural life. This must entail a dramatic land reform programme to transfer land from the inefficient, debt-ridden, ecologically-damaging and white-dominated large farm sector to all those who wish to produce incomes through farming in a more sustainable agricultural system. It also entails access to affordable services, and the promotion of non-agricultural activities. In the 'homelands', where most rural people live, social services and infrastructure remain poorly developed, and this must be remedied.

4.3.9.   Development efforts must address the special position of women, as they make up the majority of small-scale farmers, and bear the brunt of poverty, overcrowding and hunger in rural areas. They take responsibility for all aspects of their families' lives, including the need to obtain food, fuel and water, often over long distances, but are excluded from decision-making structures. They are the bulk of the seasonal labour force in agriculture, but receive the lowest wages. Their priorities include accessible water, sewage disposal, infrastructure, land rights, housing, training, local development committees, a disaster relief fund, markets for their production, and good representation in local government.

4.3.10. To correct the history of underfunding, misuse of resources and corruption, substantial transfers of funds from the central government to the rural areas will be required, targeted to meet the needs of the rural poor. The democratic government must institute a land reform process that allows people in the rural areas access to land for production and residence. It must support part-time activities, including small-scale farming, which can increase productivity, incomes and household food security. It must end the inequitable and inefficient subsidisation of the large farm sector.

4.3.11.   Rural communities need practical access to health, education, support for entrepreneurship (including agriculture), financial services, welfare, and police and the courts. The objective of rural development policy must be to coordinate the activities of the relevant democratic government agents, and to pass much of the control of democratic government-funded services to the rural people for whom they are intended, within the framework of national and provincial policy in each sector. This will require fundamental changes to institutions and processes.

4.3.12.   We must establish democratic structures to control the finances for local development activities. Elected councillors must replace the non-representative Regional Service Councils and Joint Service Boards at the district and local level.

4.3.13.   Generally, the democratic government must support capacity-building in the District Councils, Local Councils, and voluntary community structures such as local development forums. To advise communities of their options, it must train a cadre of Community Development Officers. Their training must include sensitivity to gender issues. The Community Development Officers must work for the District Councils. Wherever possible, they must come from the areas they serve.

4.3.14.   Educational opportunities in the rural areas lag far behind those in the cities. Human resource development forms a key component in building the rural economy. It must include the opening up and reorganisation of agricultural schools to meet the needs of the majority. Training and retraining of new and existing extension workers, community development officers and officials dealing with land reform are critical to the success of our rural development and land reform programme. These training and retraining programmes must be designed within the first 18 months of the RDP.

4.3.15.   The democratic government must include a central Ministry of Rural Development and Land Reform. The Ministry must include a unit for rural data collection and an early warning system for food and water security.

4.3.16. **Urban development.** The importance of urban development strategies within the RDP is based on a recognition that the urban areas account for over 80 per cent of the country's gross domestic product (GDP), and accommodate approximately 60 per cent of South Africa's population. Continuing demographic shifts may increase urbanisation to over 70 per cent of the population by 2000. The three major metropolitan areas (the PWV, Greater Cape Town and Durban) account for 37,7 per cent of the total population and 67,7 per cent of the country's total manufacturing output. The PWV region alone accounts for 40 per cent of the country's total economic output.

4.3.17. Even with a strong rural development effort, economic activities will remain concentrated in the cities. Ensuring the quality of life, sustainability and efficiency in the urban areas will thus prove critical for renewing growth and promoting equity. The design of a comprehensive national urban strategy will help serve the cities' rapidly growing populations and address the inequities and structural imbalances caused by the apartheid system. The urban development strategy must also be aimed at fostering the long-term development and sustainability of urban areas while alleviating poverty and encouraging economic expansion.

4.3.18. The urban programme must therefore have several dimensions. It must create a functionally integrated, efficient and equitable urban economy, as well as effective and democratic structures of urban governance and management; enhance the position of women in the cities, and initiate a social environment which contributes to a better quality of life.

4.3.19. Sustainable economic expansion must redress the imbalances in infrastructure, transportation and basic services in our cities. Housing, transport, electrification and other infrastructure and service programmes should promote access to employment opportunities and urban resources, and the consequent densification and unification of the urban fabric. In particular, sites for industries and services that will not harm the environment should be located near existing townships. New low-income housing should be situated near employment opportunities wherever possible.

4.3.20. The environmental impact of urban reconstruction and development must form an integral part of an urban development strategy. This includes the encroachment of urban development on viable agricultural land, air pollution, water pollution and waste management.

4.4 INDUSTRY, TRADE AND COMMERCE

4.4.1. Our economy requires coordinated and effective policies that combine private sector initiatives and government support to address its structural weaknesses. Coherent strategies are required in industry, trade and commerce to meet the challenges of a changing world economy, while at the same time meeting the needs of the majority. We also require broadly accepted, well-designed programmes which minimise the costs of restructuring and change. A five per cent growth rate and the creation of 300 000 to 500 000 non-agricultural jobs per annum can be achieved within five years.

4.4.2. **Objectives of industry, trade and commerce policy.**

4.4.2.1. The key goals of our industrial strategy are a substantial increase in net national investment, especially in manufacturing, job creation and the meeting of basic needs. Through the prudent implementation of macro-economic policies such as monetary policies, and in particular such instruments as interest rates and an increase in public sector investment, gross investment in industry will increase. In general, our objective is to enhance our technological capacity to ensure that as part of the restructuring of industry, South Africa emerges as a significant exporter of manufactured goods. The industrialisation strategy aims at the promotion of a more balanced pattern of industrial development, capable of overcoming the acute over-concentration of industrial activities in certain metropolitan centres of the country.

4.4.2.2. Trade and industrial policy must respond to the demands of reconstruction and development. In particular, industrial expansion should follow from the extension of infrastructure to urban, peri-urban and rural constituencies. Some of this new demand will be met by utilising the considerable excess capacity that exists within industry. That should lower unit costs, raise productivity and foster innovation, providing a new impetus for international competitiveness.

4.4.2.3. While trade policy must introduce instruments to promote exports of manufactured goods in general, industrial policy must support and strengthen those internationally competitive industries that emerge on the basis of stronger internal linkages, meeting the needs of recon-struction and raising capacity utilisation.

4.4.2.4. Specific policies aim to expand the competitive advantage already enjoyed by the mining and capital- and energy-intensive mineral processing and chemical industries that lie at the core of the economy and which provide the bulk of the country's foreign exchange as outlined in the section on mining and minerals below.

4.4.2.5. Policy must address the constraints on those segments of manufacturing that fall outside of bulk steel, metals and chemical production. The recent GATT agreement has necessitated painful adjustment in certain quarters, and policy should aim to reduce and share out the impact of that adjustment while at the same time promoting efficiency. Substantial institutional development on a national and sectoral level is necessary for this process, as discussed in the 'Institutional reform' section below.

4.4.2.6.   The RDP must strengthen and broaden upstream and downstream linkages between the burgeoning mineral-based industries and other sub-sectors of industry. A broad range of instruments will be deployed, including closer scrutiny of pricing policies for intermediate inputs. Where conglomerate control impedes the objectives, anti-trust policies will be invoked.

4.4.2.7.   Policies must aim to reduce the gap between conglomerate control of a wide range of activities within the financial, mining and manufacturing sectors and sub-sectors, on the one hand, and the difficulties faced by small and micro enterprises in entering those sectors on the other. As outlined in the section on small and micro enterprise, instruments may include regulatory reform, supportive measures in terms of markets, credit and training, plus measures to prevent the abuse of market power.

4.4.3.   **Trade policy.**

4.4.3.1.   Given the foreign-exchange constraints on growth in South Africa, trade policies assume enormous importance. The agreements that a democratic South Africa enters into with her major trading partners will play a crucial role in future development.

4.4.3.2.   A democratic South Africa must rapidly restructure the relationships with neighbouring African countries, who import about 20 per cent of our exports. More balanced and less exploitative trade patterns will result in more mutually beneficial outcomes. That will strengthen the Southern African region in its relations with emerging global trading blocs, as discussed in the section on Southern African regional policy below.

4.4.3.3.　Tariff reductions on imports, which are a
GATT requirement, also represent a strategic
instrument for trade policy. Presently, they
are subject to negotiation within the
National Economic Forum. The government
must develop democratic and consistent
procedures for revising tariffs and export
incentives. It must simplify the tariff structure
and begin a process of reducing protection in
ways that minimise disruption to employment
and to sensitive socio-economic areas.
National agencies concerned with
international trade and tariffs must be
sensitive to the interests of the Southern
African region as a whole.

4.4.3.4.　We must develop more cost-effective
incentives schemes, designed to improve
performance and not just the volume of
exports. Trade policy strategies to promote
exports must consider ways to reduce the bias
against small and medium-sized exporters.
They should facilitate the provision of short-
term export finance to small business. Any
duplication between the trade-promotion
arms of the Department of Trade and
Industry and the private-sector South African
Foreign Trade Organisation should be
eliminated.

4.4.4.　**Institutional reform.**

4.4.4.1.　There should be a review of the functions of
government departments, particularly those
of importance to the RDP, and of the
mandates of the various parastatals and
development institutions. As they are key
structures for the successful implementation
of the RDP, such a review must be given
priority. The evaluation should identify
whether the body is appropriate and should
continue more or less in its present form, or
whether it should be significantly altered or
merged or closed down. For instance, it
should be considered whether there is an
advantage in maintaining the science

councils or whether some or all of them should be merged.

4.4.4.2.   In order to promote greater accountability in parastatals, lines of funding and reporting must be restructured to ensure that each parastatal is directly accountable to a particular ministry. This means that funding and reporting lines must be the same.

4.4.4.3.   The processes of commercialisation and privatisation of parastatals must be reviewed, to the extent that such processes are not in the public interest. This will require the elaboration of more appropriate business plans, and publication of those plans for open debate. The democratic government will reverse privatisation programmes that are contrary to the public interest.

4.4.5.   **Negotiating forums.**

4.4.5.1.   The RDP must work with existing forums, such as the NEF, the National Electricity Forum and the National Housing Forum, and must develop a more coherent and representative system on a regional and sectoral basis. These forums must continue to build consensus around industrial and trade policy. In particular, they must: address the needs of industrial sectors forced to adjust and the question of how to share the costs of adjustment; identify new economic sites of competitive advantage; develop aspects of industrial and trade policy, and deal with problems of extending infrastructure and meeting basic needs.

4.4.5.2.   The democratic government must work together with organised labour and business in the NEF to ensure coordination between macro-economic policies and trade, industrial and technology strategy. If necessary, it must restructure the NEF to ensure appropriate participation and powers.

4.4.5.3.   Coordination of issues around energy may be facilitated by a National Energy Policy Council, as an advisory body, to oversee financing in the energy sector and to set out national policies on all aspects of energy, including liquid fuels, coal, gas, electricity, nuclear power, and other forms of energy for rural and urban consumers.

4.4.6.   **The corporate sector.**

4.4.6.1.   Business can profit hugely from the new opportunities offered by economic and social changes, especially the increased engagement with regional and international trade and the development of social and economic infrastructure. To help bring about a more dynamic business environment, the democratic state must develop measures to encourage increased productive investment, greater investment in research and development, cooperation with small and micro enterprise, workplace democratisation, and more open and flexible management styles.

4.4.6.2.   The RDP will introduce strict anti-trust legislation to create a more competitive and dynamic business environment. The central objectives of such legislation are to systematically discourage the system of pyramids where they lead to over-concentration of economic power and interlocking directorships, to abolish numerous anti-competitive practices such as market domination and abuse, and to prevent the exploitation of consumers. Existing state institutions and regulations concerned with competition policy must be reviewed in accordance with the new anti-trust policy. The democratic government should establish a commission to review the structure of control and competition in the economy and develop efficient and democratic solutions. It must review existing policy and institutions with the aim of creating more widely spread control and more effective competition. To that end, it must consider changes in regulation or management in addition to anti-trust measures.

4.4.6.3.   The domination of business activities by white business and the exclusion of black people and women from the mainstream of economic activity are causes for great concern for the reconstruction and development process. A central objective of the RDP is to deracialise business ownership and control completely, through focused policies of black economic empowerment. These policies must aim to make it easier for black people to gain access to capital for business development. The democratic government must ensure that no discrimination occurs in financial institutions. State and parastatal institutions will also provide capital for the attainment of black economic empowerment objectives. The democratic government must also introduce tendering-out procedures which facilitate black economic empowerment. Special emphasis must also be placed on training, upgrading and real participation in ownership.

4.4.6.4.   Stable, consistent and predictable policies as well as a dynamic economy should create a climate conducive to foreign investment. The democratic government must ensure treatment of foreign investors equivalent to treatment of national investors. They should abide by our laws and standards (especially with respect to labour), and obtain the advantages available to all investors. The democratic government must develop policies to ensure that foreign investment creates as much employment, technological capacity and real knowledge transfer as possible, allowing greater participation by workers in decision-making.

4.4.7. **Micro, small and medium-sized enterprise.**

4.4.7.1. Small businesses, particularly those owned and operated by black entrepreneurs, must form an integral part of the national economy and economic policy. Micro producers should develop from a set of marginalised survival strategies into dynamic small enterprises that can provide a decent living for both employees and entrepreneurs. Policies to that end must focus on women, who are represented disproportionately in this sector, especially in the rural areas.

4.4.7.2. Government agencies must provide infrastructure and skills to raise incomes and create healthier working conditions in small businesses. They must protect the rights of workers, both family members and others, and provide training in productive and managerial skills.

4.4.7.3. Experience shows that four major constraints face small and micro enterprise: the lack of access to credit, markets, skills and supportive institutional arrangements. In collaboration with small-scale entrepreneurs themselves, the democratic state must develop an integrated approach to all four problems.

4.4.7.4. In the context of a supportive industrial strategy, all levels of the democratic government – central, regional and local – must where possible foster new, dynamic relationships between large, small and micro enterprises in ways that do not harm the interests of labour. As discussed in the chapter, 'Implementing the RDP', the government must require financial institutions to lend a rising share of their assets to black-owned enterprise. All levels of the state should also, as far as possible, support joint marketing strategies and technological development within the small-scale sector.

4.4.7.5.   The democratic government must rationalise and restructure existing parastatals to support small enterprise as far as their underlying purposes allow. It should reorganise the SBDC and reform the lending criteria of other agencies such as the IDC and the development corporations so that they incorporate small and micro enterprise in their plans as far as this is feasible, and end corruption and nepotism in their lending programmes.

4.4.7.6.   Local governments must review zoning and licensing regulations to end discrimination against micro and small enterprise.

4.4.7.7.   All levels of the democratic government must review their procurement policies to ensure that, where costs permit, they support small-scale enterprise. In particular, we must explore new policies on the procurement of furniture and school uniforms, which micro producers might supply. Procurement regulations must, however, require appropriate labour standards for suppliers.

4.4.7.8.   A specific programme must be established to ensure government support for women entrepreneurs. It must be easily accessible and include skills training and access to credit.

4.4.7.9.   In addition to policies to support small-scale producers in general, the micro enterprise sector requires special attention. It will benefit from measures ranging from welfare support to activities that directly enhance competitiveness. Since the majority of informal sector workers are women, all agencies set up to support the informal sector should address their needs.

4.4.7.10.   The development of social and economic infrastructure, including pre-schools, water supplies, roads and electrification, will go a long way to improving productivity.

Infrastructural programmes must therefore take the implications for micro enterprise into account.

4.4.7.11. To better serve micro enterprise, the democratic government must double the existing number of local service centres and satellites. These satellites must enable the democratic government to provide for rural women involved in small, micro and medium-sized enterprises. All training programmes for micro enterprise must provide appropriate child care.

4.4.7.12. A variety of other measures should lower the barriers to micro enterprise. Laws should be improved to allow people in this sector to collect debts. Market sites must be established and access to existing sites facilitated. Land reform initiatives must reduce the land hunger which drives more and more people into the informal sector. Finally, as a basis for sound policy-making in future, the statistical system must incorporate micro enterprises.

4.4.8. **Science and technology policy.**

4.4.8.1. Technology policy is a key component in both industrial strategy and high-quality social and economic infrastructure. It is critical for raising productivity in both small- and large-scale enterprise.

4.4.8.2. Science and technology policy should pursue the broad objectives of developing a supportive environment for innovation; reversing the decline in resources for formal science and technology efforts in both the private and public sectors; enabling appropriate sectors of the economy to compete internationally; ensuring that scientific advances translate more effectively into technological applications, including in the small and micro sector and in rural development, and humanising technology to minimise the effect on working conditions and employment.

4.4.8.3. Technology policy must support inter-firm linkages that facilitate innovation. In research and development, the democratic government should support precompetitive collaboration between local firms and public-domain efforts combining enterprises and scientific institutes.

4.4.8.4. Incentives should support expansion in technological capacity in both existing firms and new start-ups. A greater share of government initiatives which facilitate technological development, knowledge acquisition and training must directly benefit small and micro enterprise.

4.4.8.5. Girls and women should be encouraged to obtain technical and scientific skills. The Ministry of Education must establish targets in the study of science and technology in educational institutions it subsidises. Research in the science and technology arena by the democratic government, parastatals and educational institutions must cater equally to the needs of women in this area.

4.4.8.6. New legislation must ensure that agreements to import foreign technology include a commitment to educate and train local labour to use, maintain and extend technology. Appropriate technology for small and medium-sized enterprises must be purchased where necessary and applicable from other developing countries. The democratic government must limit excessive payment of royalties and licence fees.

4.4.8.7. The democratic government must develop programmes to make university-based science more responsive to the needs of the majority of our people for basic infrastructure, goods and service. Scientific research should link up with technological advance in industry, commerce and services and in small and micro production. In particular, there must be research into appropriate and sustainable technologies for the rural areas.

4.4.8.8. The democratic government must redirect military/strategic production to civilian production. Policies should encourage former employees to develop spin-offs.

4.4.8.9. The democratic government must develop extensive institutional support and enhance government capacities to ensure successful research foresight. Because science and technology play a crucial role in the RDP, a strong coordinating agency in government must maintain on-going consultation with key stakeholders.

4.4.9. **Commerce and distribution.**

4.4.9.1. Distribution patterns have been severely distorted by apartheid and, in the last two decades, by particular investment patterns. Problems have emerged, including the biased location of distribution outlets, a distorted relationship between property investment and shopping malls, and excessive concentration of ownership, particularly in the link with the large conglomerates and in racial composition.

4.4.9.2. These issues must be addressed in order to achieve more geographically balanced and accessible distribution, lowered costs of distribution, modernised linkages between production and distribution, and greater participation by black people in the distribution chain.

4.5 RESOURCE-BASED INDUSTRIES

4.5.1. Mining and minerals.

4.5.1.1. South Africa is one of the world's richest countries in terms of minerals. Up to now, however, this enormous wealth has only been used for the benefit of the tiny white minority.

4.5.1.2. The minerals in the ground belong to all South Africans, including future generations. Moreover, the current system of mineral rights prevents the optimal development of mining and the appropriate use of urban land. We must seek the return of private mineral rights to the democratic government, in line with the rest of the world. This must be done in full consultation with all stakeholders.

4.5.1.3. Our principal objective is to transform mining and mineral-processing industries to serve all of our people. We can achieve this goal through a variety of government interventions, incentives and disincentives. Estimates suggest that the establishment of a government minerals marketing auditors' office and the national marketing of certain minerals would enable South Africa to realise greater foreign-exchange earnings. The management and marketing of our mineral exports must be examined together with employers, unions and the government to ensure maximum benefits for our country.

4.5.1.4. Minerals and mineral products are our most important source of foreign exchange and the success of our RDP will in part depend on the ability of this sector to expand exports to avoid balance of payments constraints in the short to medium term.

4.5.1.5. Mining and minerals products contribute three-quarters of our exports and the industry employs three-quarters of a million workers, but this could be much higher if our raw materials were processed into intermediate and finished products before export. Our RDP must attempt to increase the level of mineral beneficiation through appropriate incentives and disincentives in order to increase employment and add more value to our natural resources before export. Moreover, this policy should provide more appropriate inputs for manufacturing in South Africa.

4.5.1.6.   Minerals are a vital input for numerous mineral-based industries. These industries, however, have difficulty in becoming internationally competitive due to the fact that the refining companies usually set higher prices for the domestic market than their export prices, a practice known as import parity pricing. A democratic government must consider mechanisms to encourage companies to sell to local industries at prices that will enhance their international competitiveness.

4.5.1.7.   Existing tripartite structures such as the Mining Summit must be strengthened in order to facilitate national development strategies for the mining and mineral-processing industry.

4.5.1.8.   Democratisation of the mining sector must involve new laws to build workplace democracy for miners by requiring employers to negotiate the organisation of work with their employees and their unions. Programmes must be established to allow financial participation by workers in mining companies in a meaningful way (including measures to influence the policies of financial institutions, especially insurance companies and pension funds, which hold significant stakes in the mining sector and in which our people have substantial investments). And anti-trust legislation and other measures must be implemented to permit the monitoring and appropriate control of mining, mineral processing and marketing.

4.5.1.9. International demand and supply patterns for metals and minerals have undergone fundamental changes in recent years that necessitate the restructuring of this major industry. In the medium term, this probably means a continued decline in the number of people employed in the mines. Up to now, the heaviest burdens associated with down-scaling have been borne by miners, one third of whom have been retrenched. The RDP must put into place mechanisms to ensure orderly down-scaling of our mines so as to minimise the suffering of workers and their families. Measures should include the reskilling and training of workers for other forms of employment.

4.5.1.10. Mining is a hard and dangerous job, and mineworkers labour under stressful conditions, often deep under the earth. The RDP envisages a new set of minimum standards for the mining industry that ensure fair wages and employment conditions for all workers and a health and safety system that recognises the special hazards related to mining.

4.5.1.11. Most mineworkers are forced to live in single-sex hostels and remit part of their salaries. In future all workers must have the right to live at or near their place of work in decent accommodation and shall have full control over their after-tax salaries. In addition, the mining companies must take some responsibility for the education, training and social needs of miners and their families as an integral part of labour policy on the mines.

4.5.1.12. Mining can be extremely destructive of our natural environment. Our policy is to make the companies that reap the profits from mining responsible for all environmental damage. Existing legislation must be strengthened to ensure that our environment is protected. Before a new mine can be established there must be a comprehensive environmental impact study.

4.5.1.13. The Southern African region also has enormous mineral resources that have not been mined, due in part to the destabilisation policies pursued by the apartheid state in the last twenty years. In the spirit of mutual cooperation, the RDP should extend across our borders by using our considerable expertise in mineral exploration and exploitation to rehabilitate and develop the mineral potential of our neighbours. In this regard a special facility should be created to promote investment in the sub-continent.

4.5.1.14. The government must consider ways and means to encourage small-scale mining and enhance opportunities for participation by our people through support, including financial and technical aid and access to mineral rights. However, standards in respect of the environment, health and safety and other working conditions must be maintained.

4.5.2. **Agriculture.**

4.5.2.1. A vibrant and expanded agricultural sector is a critical component of a rural development and land reform programme. Agriculture contributes five per cent of GDP and over 10 per cent of employment. Sixty-six per cent of its output is in the form of intermediates and its forward and backward linkages are high. The industry is characterised by a high degree of concentration in the hands of 60 000 white farmers who own over 87 per cent of the land and produce more than 90 per cent of its product. Agriculture in the bantustans is starved of resources.

4.5.2.2. For every additional unit of capital invested, agriculture ultimately yields a larger number of job opportunities than all other sectors, with the exception of construction. The RDP aims to create a restructured agricultural sector that spreads the ownership base, encourages small-scale agriculture, further develops the commercial sector and increases production and employment. Agriculture should be oriented towards the provision of affordable food to meet the basic needs of the population and towards household food security. The pursuit of national food self-sufficiency proves too expensive and will not meet these aims. Moreover, it could undermine trade with neighbouring countries better able to produce foodstuffs.

4.5.2.3. The present commercial agricultural sector will remain an important provider of food and fibre, jobs and foreign exchange. The RDP must provide a framework for improving its performance by removing unnecessary controls and levies as well as unsustainable subsidies.

4.5.2.4. Support services provided by the democratic government, including marketing, finance and access to cooperatives, must concentrate on small and resource-poor farmers, especially women. This requires a shift from the current pattern of expensive and inefficient support for commercial farmers, as well as reform of the marketing boards and agricultural cooperatives.

4.5.2.5. Comprehensive measures should be introduced to improve the living and working conditions of farm workers. All labour legislation must be extended to farm workers, with specific provisions relating to their circumstances.

4.5.2.6.   Efficient, labour-intensive and sustainable methods of farming must be researched and promoted. To this end, extension workers should be trained and retrained and the agricultural education and research institutions restructured. The RDP must support effective drought management by providing agro-meteorological advice to farmers rather than subsidising losses, which in the past encouraged environmentally destructive farming methods.

4.5.2.7.   Increased attention must be paid to additional processing and value-adding activities derived from agriculture. This is linked to modernising marketing and exporting activities, and to the considerable potential for supplying a growing tourist industry.

4.5.3.   **Fisheries and forestry.**

4.5.3.1.   The marine resources along the South African coastline form the basis of a fishing industry which employs some 26 000 persons. The industry, however, is concentrated in the hands of a few major companies which own not only the harvesting rights, but also the processing and marketing concerns. In general wages are low, work is very often seasonal and provides little security, and it is dangerous. In addition, some fish stocks have been overexploited.

4.5.3.2.   The primary objective of fisheries policy is the upliftment of impoverished coastal communities through improved access to marine resources and the sustainable management of those resources through appropriate strategies.

4.5.3.3.   The administration of fisheries should be transferred from the Department of Environmental Affairs to a Department of Agriculture, Forestry and Fisheries. The Sea Fisheries Advisory Committee and the Quota

Board should be retained, but their membership and functions should be revised. For inshore fisheries and monitoring of catches, there should be greater community involvement in enforcement. For offshore resources, consideration must be given to establishing a regional 'Coastguard' involving the Southern African Development Community countries.

4.5.3.4. Policies must also enhance the potential for inland fisheries to improve the livelihood of rural communities through fish farming.

4.5.3.5. The RDP recognises the vast potential of the wood-based industries in South Africa. Given that the state owns almost a third of South Africa's commercial forests, the democratic government has a special responsibility to manage the development of this sector. Forests use important tracts of land, they limit the water supply in some areas, and there are potential environmental hazards in single-crop plantations such as commercial forests. The current usage of timber resources is wasteful, and we are opposed to the massive and growing export of raw wood-chips.

4.5.3.6. For these reasons the RDP promotes the tightening of regulations governing land use in sensitive areas. There is enormous scope to add value to our raw timber materials prior to export. The local pulp and paper industry can meet the growing need for paper, especially as education expands. But the price of paper products must be lowered to the benefit of local consumers as well as to enable more effective competition in international markets for value-added paper products. To achieve this, we must improve efficiency and make substantial investments. The trade unions have a significant contribution to make in restructuring this industry and enhancing its performance.

4.5.4. Tourism.

4.5.4.1.   Tourism in South Africa has been geared essentially to the local white and overseas markets, and has been adversely affected by apartheid and the resultant sanctions. All aspects of tourism were provided on a racial basis, including infrastructure, lodgings, and even national parks, game reserves and recreational areas. Natural resources are part of our national patrimony and we must develop a culture of appreciation.

4.5.4.2.   A process of reconstruction and development must take place within tourism in view of the distortions created by apartheid. In the process of restructuring, a vast potential could be realised, both in terms of the local mass market, and in terms of increased foreign exchange. This would also result in the creation of large numbers of sustainable jobs in tourism and allied industries, and would take advantage of South Africa's extraordinary human and natural resources.

4.5.4.3.   To achieve the desirable results, sound planning is needed, which should be predicated on thorough research and consultation. With respect to the local mass market, education, access to facilities and the support of black entrepreneurship are critical. In addition, promotion of ecotourism and enhancement of South Africa's unique cultural and political heritage must be prioritised. These afford opportunities for integrating traditional knowledge into tourism.

4.5.4.4.   Community involvement in tourism projects must be encouraged, stressing partnerships with other agencies and initiation and ownership of enterprises. Communities must be given access to finance, management skills, upgrading of tourist service skills, language proficiency and connections with marketing infrastructure. Training institutions should be located in areas accessible to local communities to prevent leakage of skills from the area. This could be combined with other extension services and development training programmes at regional and local level.

4.5.4.5. The Southern African dimension offers enormous tourist potential. A coordinated, mutually-beneficial policy within the region could offer some of the world's greatest natural and recreational tourist attractions.

4.5.4.6. Tourism is potentially a major source of employment and foreign exchange, and could ease balance of payments constraints in a short period of time, provided that resources required for the tourism industry are locally sourced. This requires tourism to be carefully integrated into provincial and local-level development programmes.

4.5.4.7. Without effective support from the democratic government, communities and hospitality industry workers, however, there is a danger that tourism will have potentially damaging effects on our rich and diverse cultures and natural resources. Full and transparent environmental impact assessments should be conducted for all major tourism projects. The tourism industry could be a major industry, and thus should receive greater priority at national and provincial levels.

4.6 UPGRADING INFRASTRUCTURE

4.6.1. The link between meeting basic needs through an infrastructural programme and reviving economic growth in manufacturing and other sectors is the essence of the link between reconstruction and development. However, it is more than just providing electricity, water and telecommunications. It is a programme that integrates and upgrades infrastructure at the same time.

4.6.2.   The infrastructural programme must ensure an integrated approach to the provision of various services so that we upgrade our infrastructure in a manner that both meets basic needs and enhances new and effective economic activity. This is particularly true in areas of information technology. Upgrading in these areas can facilitate an upgrading of education, health care, recreation and other services, by improving the quality of information available and providing communities throughout the country with access to expertise and usable data.

4.6.3.   The use of information technology provides a major challenge in linking basic needs with information highways in innovative ways that improve the capacity of industry to successfully reintegrate into world markets. Southern Africa could lead the way in providing this link so vital to the developing world.

4.6.4.   In addition to upgrading infrastructure in existing areas, its extension to all parts of the sub-continent will both break down apartheid and colonial geography, and open up new economic potential in the areas of production and tourism.

4.6.5.   **Electrification.** In addition to meeting basic energy and lighting needs for households, specific attention must be paid to making electricity available to micro, small, medium-sized and agricultural enterprises in both urban and rural areas. The benefits of cheap electricity presently enjoyed by large corporations must be extended to all parts of the economy.

4.6.6.   **Telecommunications.** Under apartheid, telecommunications were not developed in a manner cognisant of the possibilities for expanding the economy to the lives of all South Africans. As a result, massive inefficiencies and missed opportunities characterise the sector. Information is today considered a commodity of great significance, and South Africa must now catch-up in order to take advantage of the changing technological and economic roles that telecommunications can play.

4.6.7.   The development of an advanced information network should play a crucial role in facilitating the provision of high-quality services to all the people of South Africa. It must provide a significant advantage to the business sector as it reduces costs and increases productivity, and serves as an integral part of financial services, the commodities market, trade and manufacturing.

4.6.8. The basic infrastructural network must remain within the public sector. Certain value-added services could be licensed within the framework of an overall telecommunications programme. An integrated system of groundline, microwave, fibre-optic and satellite communications must substantially enhance the overall system.

4.6.9. The RDP aims to bring telecommunications closer to all potential users. A telecommunications regulatory authority must be established, which should be separated from policy and operating activities.

4.6.10. The development of telecommunications must be underpinned by a strong telecommunications manufacturing sector. The democratic government must encourage this sector to work closely with the network operators in developing suitable systems for possible export to Africa and other developing areas.

4.6.11. **Transport.** There is an urgent need to develop an integrated and rapid transportation system that links the domestic economy, Southern Africa, and world markets. This entails the upgrading of road and rail networks and their extension to the whole area, but also a rapid interface between road, rail, air and sea.

4.6.12. A review of the current situation within all transportation systems must be undertaken in order to assess the capacity of these systems and how they could enhance the development of other sectors of the economy and contribute to the RDP. The structure of the railway network and its operating system was badly distorted by our colonial and apartheid history. A comprehensive review of both the network and operating system is needed to increase their contribution to the RDP. A similar review is required in road freight with particular attention being paid to ownership patterns and barriers to entry. Particular attention must be paid to the regulatory structures of the transportation systems.

4.6.13. A Southern African transportation network enhanced by information networks could play a major role in underpinning the socio-economic reconstruction of the sub-continent.

4.7 REFORM OF THE FINANCIAL SECTOR

4.7.1. The apartheid system severely distorted the South African financial system. A handful of large financial institutions, all linked closely to the dominant conglomerates, centralise most of the country's financial assets. But they prove unable to serve most of the black community, especially women. Nor do they contribute significantly to the development of new sectors of the economy. Small informal-sector institutions meet some of the needs of the black community and micro enterprise. They lack the resources, however, to bring about broad-scale development.

4.7.2. **The regulatory framework**. The democratic government must modify regulations and support innovative financial institutions and instruments which mobilise private domestic savings to help fund the RDP, while not reducing incentives for personal savings. The democratic government must enhance accountability, access and transparency in the financial sector. In cooperation with other stakeholders, it must review both regulations and regulatory system to determine which aspects prove an unnecessary impediment to the RDP, and more generally to greater efficiency in the mobilisation and subsequent allocation of savings. Government must encourage the private sector to cooperate in extending financial services to those who presently do not have access to these services. The establishment of a smoothly functioning and inexpensive payments system, assuring safety of consumer deposits, must be considered a high priority. To improve flexibility in the legal environment, parliament should establish an oversight committee for the financial sector.

4.7.3.   **Prohibition against discrimination.** The democratic
government must introduce measures to combat
discrimination on the grounds of race, gender, location
and other non-economic factors. The democratic
government must, in consultation with financial
institutions, establish prudent non-discriminatory
lending criteria, especially in respect of
creditworthiness and collateral; reform the laws on
women and banking to ensure equality; forbid blanket
bans on mortgage bonds to specific communities
('redlining'); require banks to give their reasons when
turning down a loan application; establish community
liaison boards; develop simpler forms for contracts and
applications, and create an environment which reduces
the risk profile of lending to small black-owned
enterprises and requires banks to lend a rising share of
their assets to small, black-owned enterprise. The law
must also require that financial institutions disclose
their loans by race and gender; their assets and
liabilities by subregion and sector; their staff by race
and gender; the location of their branches and defaults
by neighbourhood. To enforce laws against
discrimination, the democratic government must
establish an ombuds for the financial sector. At the
local level, ombuds structures must include community
representatives. Where anti-discrimination measures do
not generate enough credit for housing, small
enterprise and other RDP programmes, the government
must provide appropriate kinds of financial support.
The democratic government should consider reapplying
the Usury Act to small loans (in addition to loans above
R6 000, as presently applies), and should enforce the
Act more effectively.

4.7.4.   **Housing bank and guarantee fund**. The democratic
government must establish a Housing Bank to ensure
access to wholesale finance for housing projects and
programmes. A Guarantee Fund will protect private
sector funds from undue risk. Approximately half the
Bank's funds will come from the government in the form
of recurrent housing subsidies, in order to ensure
affordable bonds.

4.7.5.   **Community banking**. Community banks of various
types have proven able to finance informal
entrepreneurs, especially women. The democratic

government must encourage community banking. It must reform regulations to foster the development of community banks while protecting customers. Where possible, government structures at all levels should conduct business with these institutions. The government must encourage the established banks and other financial institutions to help fund the community banks.

4.7.6.   **Pension and mutual funds**. Pension and provident funds should be made more accountable to their members, and insurance companies to their contributors. The democratic government must change the law to ensure adequate representation for workers through the trade unions and compulsory contributions by employers, and move towards industry funds. It must also legislate a transformation of the boards of the Mutual Funds to make them more socially responsible. The RDP must embark on a review of financial institution legislation, regulation and supervision to ensure the protection of pension and provident funds and other forms of savings and investment.

4.7.7.   **The Reserve Bank**. The Interim Constitution contains several mechanisms which ensure that the Reserve Bank is both insulated from partisan interference and accountable to the broader goals of development and maintenance of the currency. In addition, the law must change the Act governing the Reserve Bank to ensure a board of directors that can better serve society as a whole. The board must include representatives from the trade unions and civil society. In future, a stronger board of governors should emerge through the appointment of better-qualified individuals. The new constitutional requirement that the board of governors record its decisions, publicise them when feasible, and account to parliament should help in developing a more professional and credible executive, with greater ability to exercise its mandate than the present board of governors.

4.7.8.   The democratic government should immediately increase the resources available in the Reserve Bank and other appropriate agencies for combating illegal capital flight. Furthermore, the democratic government must enter into discussions with holders of wealth in an

effort to persuade them of the harmful effects their
actions are having on our economy.

4.8 LABOUR AND WORKER RIGHTS

4.8.1.   Over the years, workers have won many struggles and
made many gains in the workplace. The fundamental
principle of the RDP is to safeguard these rights and
extend them. Organised labour must be empowered to
act as a strong force in the reconstruction and
development of our country.

4.8.2.   There must be equal rights for all workers, embodied in
a single set of labour statutes.

4.8.3.   **Basic organising rights**. The following rights of
workers must be in the Constitution:

4.8.3.1.   the right to organise and join trade unions;

4.8.3.2.   the right to strike and picket on all economic
and social matters, and

4.8.3.3.   the right to information from companies and
the government.

4.8.4.   The Constitution should not prohibit the conclusion of
union security agreements, including closed and agency
shops. The right to lock out should not be in the
Constitution.

4.8.5.   **Living wage.** All workers should be entitled to a living
wage and humane conditions of employment in a
healthy and safe working environment. The
interlocking elements of the RDP, in particular the
promotion of collective bargaining, minimum wage
regulation, affirmative action, education and training,
technological development, and provision of services
and social security, must all be combined to achieve a
living wage for rural and urban workers and reduce
wage differentials. The required levels of growth for
the successful implementation of the RDP can only be
achieved on the basis of living wage policies agreed
upon by government, the labour movement and the
private sector.

4.8.6.   Reconstructing and developing the economy require far-reaching changes in employment patterns and labour market policies. The democratic government must set up institutions and mechanisms to facilitate this process in order to avoid unnecessary hardships while utilising our human resources to their full potential.

4.8.7.   **Collective bargaining.** Effective implementation of the RDP requires a system of collective bargaining at national, industrial and workplace level, giving workers a key say in industry decision-making and ensuring that unions are fully involved in designing and overseeing changes at workplace and industry levels.

4.8.8.   Industrial bargaining forums or industrial councils must play an important role in the implementation of the RDP. Agreements negotiated in such forums should be extended through legislation to all workplaces in that industry. There must be enhanced jurisdiction for these forums to negotiate:

4.8.8.1.   industrial policy including the implementation of the RDP at sectoral level;

4.8.8.2.   training and education programmes;

4.8.8.3.   job placement programmes in the industry, and

4.8.8.4.   job creation programmes.

4.8.9.   **Workplace empowerment.** Legislation must facilitate worker participation and decision-making in the world of work. Such legislation must include an obligation on employers to negotiate substantial changes concerning production matters or workplace organisation within a nationally negotiated framework, facilities for organisation and communication with workers on such matters, and the right of shop stewards to attend union meetings and training without loss of pay as well as to address workers.

4.8.10.   In addition to the reform of labour law, company and tax law must be amended to ensure that the rights of workers are protected and extended, for example in relation to workers' access to company information.

4.8.11. Instruments of policy such as subsidies, taxes, tariffs, tenders etc. must all be utilised to encourage stakeholder participation in the RDP and promote worker rights, human resource development and job creation.

4.8.12. Since human resource development is crucial to the successful implementation of the RDP, the democratic government must support programmes to upgrade skills on a broad basis in terms of a national education and training policy negotiated between unions, employers and government. Further details are set out in Chapter Three.

4.8.13. **Affirmative action.** Affirmative action measures must be used to end discrimination on the grounds of race and gender, and to address the disparity of power between workers and management, and between urban and rural areas. Those measures must:

   4.8.13.1. entail a massive programme of education, training, retraining, adult basic education and recognition of prior learning, to overcome the legacy of apartheid;

   4.8.13.2. empower not only individuals, but communities and groups, under conditions which promote the collective rights and capacity of workers and their representatives to negotiate workplace issues;

   4.8.13.3. establish principles for the hiring and the promotion of workers with similar skills/jobs which will prevent discrimination against people previously disadvantaged by apartheid or gender;

   4.8.13.4. accelerate, through collective bargaining programmes, the eradication of discrimination in each and every workplace;

   4.8.13.5. provide job security for pregnant women and promote the provision of child care, as discussed in Chapter Three, to further women's equality in employment;

4.8.13.6. ensure that the development of special expertise among South Africans takes priority over the import of outside personnel (this policy should not, however, prejudice foreign investment or cooperation in the Southern African region), and

4.8.13.7. establish legislation and a strong ombuds to monitor and implement affirmative action measures.

4.8.14. Legislation must prohibit sexual harassment, and education programmes must be launched to make workers and employers aware about the issue and about how to lodge complaints.

4.8.15. **International conventions.** The international labour conventions of the International Labour Organisation (ILO) concerning freedom of association, collective bargaining, workplace representation and other fundamental rights must be ratified by the South African government.

4.8.16. **Restructuring of labour market institutions.** The Department of Manpower and labour market institutions related to it, such as the Unemployment Insurance Board, and the Workmen's Compensation Board, must be restructured in consultation with the major stakeholders in the tripartite labour market forums such as the National Manpower Commission.

4.8.17. All of the above, coupled with a democratic political dispensation, improvements in the living standards of workers and a programme of human resource development will release the resources of the nation's workers and significantly improve productivity in the economy.

4.9 SOUTHERN AFRICAN REGIONAL POLICY

4.9.1. In the long run, sustainable reconstruction and development in South Africa requires sustainable reconstruction and development in Southern Africa as a whole. Otherwise, the region will face continued high unemployment and underemployment, leading to labour migration and brain drain to the more industrialised areas. The democratic government must negotiate with neighbouring countries to forge an equitable and mutually beneficial programme of increasing cooperation, coordination and integration appropriate to the conditions of the region. In this context, the RDP must support the goals and ideals of African integration as laid out in the Lagos Plan of Action and the Abuja Declaration.

4.9.2.   Whilst South Africa's trade with its neighbours in Southern Africa constitutes a relatively small percentage of its total trade with the world, this trade has been growing rapidly over the past few years. In addition, a significant percentage of South Africa's exports to African countries that are not members of the Southern African Customs Union (SACU) consists of manufactured goods. Various studies have shown that there is a great complementarity between the types of goods imported by Southern African Development Community (SADC) and Preferential Trade Area (PTA) countries and the goods that South Africa is exporting.

4.9.3.   However, the current trade pattern between South Africa and the sub-continent is unbalanced, as regional imports from South Africa exceed exports to South Africa by five to one. A democratic government must develop policies in consultation with our neighbours to ensure more balanced trade.

4.9.4.   Developing the capacity of our neighbours to export manufactured goods to South African markets requires the democratic government, in consultation with neighbouring states, to encourage and promote industrial development throughout the region. A democratic government must contribute towards the development of regional and industrial strategies for specific sub-sectors, such as mineral beneficiation, auto components and textiles.

4.9.5.   A democratic government should also encourage the development of joint, mutually-beneficial projects to develop our regional water resources, electricity and energy supply, transport and telecommunications, and agricultural and food production.

4.9.6.   One element of regional policy, defended particularly in the call for a Southern African Social Charter by trade unions, is that minimum standards with regard to rights of workers to organise be established across the region as a whole. This will allow a process of greater integration to become one of levelling up rights and conditions of workers, rather than of levelling them down to the lowest prevailing standard.

4.9.7.   A democratic government should encourage technical and scientific cooperation with our neighbours to enhance the development of expertise in the region in areas such as agricultural research and development, environmental monitoring and protection, health and other research.

4.9.8.   A democratic South African government should apply for membership in the SADC and possibly the PTA, and should support reforms in the SACU to enhance democracy and equity. Within these structures we must enhance our capacity as a region to effectively interact with international financial and trade institutions.

5.
Democratising the State and Society

5.1 PROBLEM STATEMENT

5.1.1. The apartheid regime has been unrepresentative, undemocratic and highly oppressive. In past decades the state became increasingly secretive and militarised, and less and less answerable even to the constituency it claimed to represent.

5.1.2. The legal and institutional framework we are inheriting is fragmented and inappropriate for reconstruction and development. It lacks capacity to deliver services, it is inefficient and out of touch with the needs of ordinary people. It lacks coordination and clear planning.

5.1.3. The financing of development programmes under the apartheid state was wasteful, misdirected and mismanaged. There was corruption, and many state and development institutions carry over debts from the apartheid era with which the new government must deal.

5.1.4. Apartheid patterns of minority domination and privilege are not confined to the state and parastatals. Every aspect of South African life is deeply marked by minority domination and privilege. A vast range of institutions in the private domain (in civil society) benefitted from apartheid, and also actively fostered and sustained it.

5.2 VISION AND OBJECTIVES

5.2.1. **The People shall govern.** The RDP vision is one of democratising power. Democracy is intimately linked to reconstruction and development. We will not be able to unleash the resources, neglected skills and stunted potential of our country and its people while minority domination of state and civil institutions persists. Without thoroughgoing democratisation, the whole effort to reconstruct and develop will lose momentum. Reconstruction and development require a population that is empowered through expanded rights, meaningful information and education, and an institutional network fostering representative, participatory and direct democracy.

5.2.2.   Democracy requires that all South Africans have access to power and the right to exercise their power. This will ensure that all people will be able to participate in the process of reconstructing our country.

5.2.3.   Empowerment means, in the first place, the enfranchisement of all South Africans – one person, one vote – and the extension of equal citizenship rights to all. Deepening democracy will require ensuring that elected structures conduct themselves in an answerable and transparent manner. Clear Codes of Conduct must be established and enforced for all public representatives.

5.2.4.   Democratisation requires modernising the structures and functioning of government in pursuit of the objectives of efficient, effective, responsive, transparent and accountable government. We must develop the capacity of government for strategic intervention in social and economic development. We must increase the capacity of the public sector to deliver improved and extended public services to all the people of South Africa.

5.2.5.   The defence force and the police and intelligence services must be transformed from being agents of oppression into effective servants of the community, with the capacity to participate in the RDP. Our society must be thoroughly demilitarised and all security forces under clear civilian control.

5.2.6.   Democracy for ordinary citizens must not end with formal rights and periodic one-person, one-vote elections. Without undermining the authority and responsibilities of elected representative bodies (the national assembly, provincial legislatures, local government), the democratic order we envisage must foster a wide range of institutions of participatory democracy in partnership with civil society on the basis of informed and empowered citizens (e.g. the various sectoral forums like the National Economic Forum) and facilitate direct democracy (people's forums, referenda where appropriate, and other consultation processes).

5.2.7. A wide range of trade unions, mass organisations, other sectoral movements and community-based organisations (CBOs) such as civic associations developed in our country in opposition to apartheid oppression. These social movements and CBOs are a major asset in the effort to democratise and develop our society. Attention must be given to enhancing the capacity of such formations to adapt to partially changed roles. Attention must also be given to extending social-movement and CBO structures into areas and sectors where they are weak or non-existent.

5.2.8. Numerous non-profit non-governmental organisations (NGOs) are also developing in South Africa. Many of these NGOs play an important capacity-building role in regard to CBOs and the development process. NGOs are also engaged in service delivery, mobilisation, advocacy, planning, lobbying, and financing. Thus NGOs have an important future role in the democratisation of our society. However, NGOs must also adopt transparent processes, and operate in a manner that responds, with accountability and democracy, to the communities they serve.

5.2.9. Deepening democracy in our society is not only about various governmental and non-governmental institutions. Effective democracy implies and requires empowered citizens. Formal rights must be given real substance. All of the social and economic issues (like job creation, housing and education) addressed in previous chapters of the RDP are directly related to empowering our people as citizens. One further area is absolutely central in this regard – a democratic information programme.

5.2.10. Ensuring gender equity is another central component in the overall democratisation of our society. The RDP envisages special attention being paid to the empowerment of women in general, and of black, rural women in particular. There must be representation of women in all institutions, councils and commissions, and gender issues must be included in the terms of reference of these bodies.

5.3 CONSTITUENT ASSEMBLY

5.3.1.   The new Constitution should be drawn up by the Constituent Assembly in an open and transparent manner. The new Constitution must reinforce the RDP, ensuring that equality of rights of citizens is not just formal, but substantive. The new Constitution should ensure that social, economic, environmental and peace rights are more fully embodied in the Bill of Rights.

5.3.2.   The Constitution must recognise the fundamental equality of men and women in marriage, employment and in society. There should be a continuous review of all legislation to ensure that this clause in the Constitution is not undermined. These principles must override customary law. Consideration should be given to the implementation of a constitutional provision for the calling of a referendum in order to overturn unpopular laws, and to ensure that certain laws get passed.

5.3.3.   The Constitution should permit the regulation of the use of property when this is in the public interest. It should also guarantee a right to restitution for victims of forced removals.

5.3.4.   The Constitution should provide for sufficient central government powers so as to coordinate and implement the RDP effectively.

5.4 NATIONAL AND PROVINCIAL ASSEMBLIES

5.4.1.   The National and Provincial Assemblies must establish legislation and programmes which ensure substantive equality rather than formal equality.

5.4.2.   There should be a review of the legislative procedures including a review of national and regional parliamentary sessions, operating procedures and the composition of standing committees, to promote an improved institutional framework for public decision-making. There should be a clear right of access to the parliamentary legislative procedures to allow inputs from interested parties. There should be a Code of Conduct for members of the National and Regional Assemblies.

5.5 NATIONAL AND PROVINCIAL GOVERNMENT

5.5.1.   South Africa has been divided into nine provinces. These provinces are at different levels of development and are not equally endowed with resources. The existing constitutional arrangements provided for by the Interim Constitution require that provincial levels of government and the national government develop methods for working closely together to ensure the implementation of the RDP. This will ensure that development in all these areas takes place evenly throughout the country and that minimum standards are attained.

5.5.2.   Grants-in-aid strategies must be built into the RDP to ensure that all provinces receive an equitable share of revenue collected nationally. The Financial and Fiscal Commission must determine criteria for the allocation of inter-governmental grants.

5.5.3.   The reincorporation of the TBVC states (Transkei, Bophuthatswana, Venda, Ciskei) and the self-governing territories requires urgent attention. All government departments at national level must be rationalised to end duplications due to racial divisions. Single ministries should be created at national and provincial level in each sector of operation. At the provincial level, government institutions must be constructed and rationalised out of existing regional structures. The role, function and mission of government departments should be reviewed with the aim of introducing a clear development focus for the democratic government administration. Policies of affirmative action, development and training must be applied in all areas.

5.6 SECURITY FORCES

5.6.1.   The defence force, the police and intelligence services must be firmly under civilian control, in the first place through the relevant civilian ministry answerable to parliament. These security forces must uphold the democratic constitution, they must be non-partisan, and they must be bound by clear codes of conduct.

5.6.2.   The size, character and doctrines of the new defence force must be appropriate to a country engaged in a major programme of socio-economic reconstruction and development. The rights of soldiers must be clearly defined and protected.

5.6.3.   The police service must be transformed, with special attention to representivity, and gender and human rights sensitivity. National standards and training must be combined with community-based structures to ensure answerability to the communities served.

5.7 THE ADMINISTRATION OF JUSTICE

5.7.1.   The system of justice should be made accessible and affordable to all people. It must be credible and legitimate. The legal processes and institutions should be reformed by simplifying the language and procedures used in the court, recognising and regulating community and customary courts, and professionalising the Attorney-General's office. The public defence system must be promoted and the prosecution system reformed. The pool of judicial officers should be increased through the promotion of lay officials, scrapping the divided bar and giving the right of appearance to paralegals.

5.7.2.   The Industrial Court system should be restructured so that workers who have complaints against employers are able to have these disputes resolved in a cheap, accessible and speedy manner. Tripartite institutions should have a say in determining appointments to the Industrial and Labour Appeal Courts.

5.7.3.   A legal aid fund for women to test their rights in court must be established.

5.8 PRISONS

5.8.1. The staffing of the prison service must be based on non-racial and non-sexist principles. Prison staff will need to be trained to reflect this approach and to transform the present military command structure of the prison service.

5.8.2. Prisoners must enjoy human rights and must be fully protected by the Constitution.

5.8.3. The prison service must play its part, not simply in restraining convicted persons, but in rehabilitating and training them. Adequate resources must be made available for the humane accommodation of prisoners.

5.8.4. The law dealing with children in custody must be reformed. Practices which infringe even the existing laws (such as the accommodation of children and juvenile prisoners in cells with adults) must be ended.

5.8.5. Pregnant women and mothers with small children in prison must be held in conditions which are appropriate for their specific physical and psychological requirements.

5.8.6. Disciplinary codes within prison must be changed, and forms of punishment which infringe basic human rights (solitary confinement and dietary punishment) must be ended.

5.8.7. The public has the right to be informed about prison conditions. The Prison Act must, accordingly, be substantially reformed.

5.8.8. Prisons must be monitored by an independent prison ombuds, appointed by the State President, but working independently of ministerial control.

5.9 RESTRUCTURING THE PUBLIC SECTOR

5.9.1. South Africa has a large public sector with many resources. The public sector consists of the public service, the police and defence forces, the intelligence service, parastatals, public corporations and advisory bodies, which are together some of the most important delivery and empowerment mechanisms for the RDP. Staffing levels in and budgetary allocations to government departments and institutions must match the requirements for service delivery, and the operational requirements for women's empowerment, within the constraints of the budget. A defined quota of all new employees should come from groups that were disadvantaged on the basis of race and gender, and all employees should be given access to appropriate training and support systems. This should be evaluated each year to determine the progress made and identify problems which arise. By the turn of the century, the personnel composition of the public sector, including parastatals, must have changed to reflect the national distribution of race and gender. Such progress will enhance the full utilisation of the country's labour power and productivity.

5.10 THE PUBLIC SERVICE

5.10.1. The Public Service Commission established in terms of the Interim Constitution must be responsible for matters relating to appointments, promoting efficiency and effectiveness in departments, establishing and monitoring a Code of Conduct for the public service, and introducing a programme of affirmative action and other appropriate techniques to eliminate historical inequities in employment. The Code of Conduct must incorporate the principles of the new South African public service as outlined in the RDP. The ethos should be professional, in the most positive sense of the word; the public service must internalise the concept of 'serving the people'. This Code should be enforced and annual evaluation of personnel should take into account compliance with the Code.

5.10.2. The public service should be composed in such a way that it is capable of and committed to the implementation of the policies of the government and the delivery of basic goods and services to the people of the country. In particular, priority must be given to developing the mechanisms for implementing the policies, recommendations and directives of the restructured Public Service Commission and the RDP.

5.10.3.   While the public service must be based on merit, career principles, suitability, skills, competence and qualifications, these standards should not be interpreted to further minority interests, as in the past. An extensive programme of affirmative action must be embarked on to achieve the kind of public service that is truly reflective of our society, particularly at the level of management and senior employees. Such an affirmative action programme must include training and support to those who have previously been excluded from holding responsible positions. Within two years of the implementation of the programme, recruitment and training should reflect South African society, in terms of race, class and gender. Mechanisms must be put in place to monitor implementation of the programme. A programme of monitoring and retraining for all those willing to serve loyally under a democratic government should be instituted.

5.10.4.   The Civil Service Training Institute must be transformed to train and retrain public service employees in line with the priorities of the RDP. One of the priorities of this Institute must be to ensure that a cadre of public servants is developed to transform the public service effectively, with attention to excellence and high levels of service delivery. The Institute must be provided with the necessary resources and cater for at least four levels of training: lateral entry for progressive academics, activists, organisers and NGO workers; top-level management development; promotion within the public service, and retraining of present incumbents of posts.

5.10.5.   A sound labour relations philosophy, policy and practice is an essential requirement for building a motivated, committed cadre of personnel who have a clear vision of their development goals. Labour relations policy must also provide for dealing systematically with corruption, mismanagement and victimisation in public institutions. Labour policy must permit the participation of public sector workers and their organisations in decision-making at various levels in this sector. This will require amendment of existing labour legislation and a review of management practice in the public sector.

5.11 PARASTATALS AND STATE DEVELOPMENT INSTITUTIONS

5.11.1.   Parastatals, public corporations and advisory boards must be structured and run in a manner that reinforces and supports the RDP. Civil society must be adequately represented on the boards of parastatals and public corporations. Institutions must be transparent and open in both structure and decision-making. They should act within the framework of public policy and there must be a duty to inform the general public as well as to account to parliament.

5.11.2.   The statutory bodies must be independent of government departments in the sense that they should not be directly part of any government department. They should be controlled by general government policies and by their governance councils. The emphasis should be on creating stable long-term policies rather than volatile short-term policy. To ensure effective civil participation in these bodies, governance councils should be composed of mandated representatives of appropriate organisations, not appointed individuals.

5.11.3.   All bodies must run on full cost accounting. All subsidies paid or received must be the result of an explicit and transparent decision. In addition, parastatals which receive 20 per cent of their funding or R20 million (whichever is less) from government, should submit an annual director's report to the relevant ministry, showing how allocated funds were used given the objectives agreed to. Every ministry and parastatal should have an office that periodically reviews its activities and measures performance as well as appraising staff performance. Rationalisation of the activities and resources of parastatals should take place to promote efficiency and effectiveness. Parastatals should have a public consciousness.

5.11.4.   Control of funds set aside specifically for development purposes (be they from contracts, the democratic government or the public domain) should vest in a competent and legitimate government agency, which could include representation from civil society.

5.12 LOCAL GOVERNMENT

5.12.1. Local government is of critical importance to the RDP. It is the level of representative democracy closest to the people. Local government will often be involved in the allocation of resources directly affecting communities. Local government should be structured on a democratic, non-racial and non-sexist basis. The Local Government Transition Act provides for the start of this process with the establishment of transitional councils, and the creation of a framework for the first non-racial local government elections.

5.12.2. The constitutional and legal arrangements, which provide for councils of local unity during the transitional phase, should be removed from the final Constitution to make local government more democratic. Existing local government legislation, including the Local Government Transition Act and the Provincial Ordinances, should be amended or repealed where necessary by a competent legislative authority.

5.12.3. An estimated 800 segregated local authorities must be amalgamated into approximately 300 new local authorities with non-racial boundaries. The existing grading system for local authorities should be revised to reflect the needs of people, and not just existing consumption of services.

5.12.4. The demarcation of boundaries of local authorities should ensure that informal settlements on the outskirts of towns and cities, and urban settlements displaced behind homeland boundaries, are incorporated into the jurisdiction of new local authorities.

5.12.5. Elected local government, with responsibility for the delivery of services, should be extended into rural areas, including traditional authority areas. Rural district councils that incorporate a number of primary local councils must have a key role in rural local government.

5.12.6. In major urban centres, strong metropolitan government should be established to assist in the integration and coordination of the urban economies.

5.12.7. Separate budgets and financial systems must be integrated on the basis of 'one municipality, one tax base'. The arrears and debts of the black local authorities, estimated at R1,8 billion, should be written off by a competent legislature.

5.12.8. All local authorities should embark on programmes to restore, maintain, upgrade and extend networks of services. Within a local authority, the total body of consumers should be responsible for the cost of the service, including capital improvements, thus allowing for cross-subsidisation of new consumers. Tariff structures should be structured on a progressive basis to address problems of affordability. Within this framework, all consumers should pay for services consumed.

5.12.9. Local authorities should be assisted to deal with the existing backlog of municipal services through inter-governmental transfers from central and provincial government, according to criteria established by the Financial and Fiscal Commission.

5.12.10. Separate local authority administrations must be amalgamated, reorganised and rationalised, after consultation between employer and employee bodies. A centralised system of collective bargaining for municipal employees should be established.

5.12.11. The Training Board for Local Government Bodies should be restructured to provide more effective training for employees of local authorities. The entrance criteria of professional bodies such as the Institute of Town Clerks and the Institute of Municipal Treasurers and Accountants should be broadened to ensure better access for all South Africans to these professions.

5.12.12. At local government level a women's portfolio should be established with powers to scrutinise local authority programmes and budgets for gender sensitivity. Local authorities can play a role in the implementation of affirmative action with the private sector through special criteria for local government contracts.

5.12.13. A developmental culture among local government administrations should be encouraged. The actions of councillors and officials should be open and transparent, with councillors subject to an enforceable Code of Conduct.

5.12.14. Local authority administrations should be structured in such a way as to ensure maximum participation of civil society and communities in decision-making and developmental initiatives of local authorities.

5.13 CIVIL SOCIETY

5.13.1. Apart from the strategic role of government in the RDP, mass participation in its elaboration and implementation is essential. Within the first nine months of 1994 the RDP must be taken to People's Forums, rallies and meetings in communities.

5.13.2. In the course of 1994, trade unions, sectoral social movements and CBOs, notably civics, must be encouraged to develop RDP programmes of action and campaigns within their own sectors and communities. Many social movements and CBOs will be faced with the challenge of transforming their activities from a largely oppositional mode into a more developmental one. To play their full role these formations will require capacity-building assistance. This should be developed with democratic government facilitation and funded through a variety of sources. A set of rigorous criteria must be established to ensure that beneficiaries deserve the assistance and use it for the designated purposes. Every effort must be made to extend organisation into marginalised communities and sectors like, for instance, rural black women.

5.13.3. Trade unions and other mass organisations must be actively involved in democratic public policy-making. This should include involvement in negotiations ranging from the composition of the Constitutional Court to international trade and loan agreements. Education about trade unions and other mass organisations should also be promoted in school curricula and through publicly-funded media.

5.13.4. Delivery or enforcement mechanisms for social and economic rights must not focus only on the Constitution, courts and judicial review, but must include agencies which have the involvement of members and organisations of civil society as means of enforcing social justice. In this regard, a revamped Human Rights Commission, with wider popular involvement, should have its mandate extended to ensure that social and economic rights are being met.

5.13.5.   Institutions of civil society should be encouraged to improve their accountability to their various constituencies and to the public at large. There should be no restriction on the right of the organisations to function effectively. Measures should be introduced to create an enabling environment for social movements, CBOs and NGOs in close consultation with those bodies and to promote donations to the non-profit sector. This should include funding of Legal Advice Centres and paralegals.

5.13.6.   The rights of individual people should be protected and guaranteed in the processes of government. Groups and communities should be encouraged to contribute to the reconstruction and development process. Parents should be empowered through school governance, residents through residents' associations, etc.

5.13.7.   Multipartite policy forums (like the present National Economic Forum) representing the major role players in different sectors should be established and existing forums restructured to promote efficient and effective participation of civil society in decision-making. Such forums must exist at the national, provincial and local levels.

5.13.8.   Forums such as the National Economic Forum constitute important opportunities for organs of civil society to participate in and influence policy-making. Similarly they provide the democratic government with an important mechanism for broad consultation on policy matters. They need to be assisted (and sometimes restructured) to improve their effectiveness, representivity and accountability.

5.14 A DEMOCRATIC INFORMATION PROGRAMME

5.14.1. Open debate and transparency in government and society are crucial elements of reconstruction and development. This requires an information policy which guarantees active exchange of information and opinion among all members of society. Without the free flow of accurate and comprehensive information, the RDP will lack the mass input necessary for its success.

5.14.2. The new information policy must aim at facilitating exchange of information within and among communities and between the democratic government and society as a two-way process. It must also ensure that media play an important role in facilitating projects in such areas as education and health.

5.14.3. The democratic government must encourage the development of all three tiers of media – public, community and private. However, it must seek to correct the skewed legacy of apartheid where public media were turned into instruments of National Party policy; where community media were repressed; where private media are concentrated in the hands of a few monopolies, and where a few individuals from the white community determine the content of media. New voices at national, regional and local levels, and genuine competition rather than a monopoly of ideas, must be encouraged.

5.14.4. An affirmative action programme, consistent with the best experiences in the world, must be put into place to empower communities and individuals from previously disadvantaged sectors of society. This must include: mechanisms to make available resources needed to set up broadcasting and printing enterprises at a range of levels; training and upgrading, and civic education to ensure that communities and individuals recognise and exercise their media rights.

5.14.5. Measures must be taken to limit monopoly control of the media. Cross-ownership of print and broadcast media must be subject to strict limitations determined in a public and transparent manner. The democratic government must encourage unbundling of the existing media monopolies. This includes monopolies in the areas of publishing and distribution. Where necessary, anti-trust legislation must be brought to bear on these monopolies.

5.14.6. The democratic government must set aside funds for training of journalists and community-based media and, at the same time, encourage media institutions to do the same.

5.14.7. To ensure the free flow of information – within the broad parameters of the Bill of Rights – the Freedom of Information Act must be broadened.

5.14.8. The democratic government must have a major role to play in the introduction of a new information policy. This must, however, be limited to facilitation rather than dabbling in the editorial content of media enterprises. Further, a deliberate policy must be followed to prevent unwarranted state intervention in levelling the media playing field or in preserving privileged status for government information. The Bill of Rights and, if necessary, legislation will be crucial in this regard.

5.14.9. The South African Communications Services (SACS) must be restructured in order to undertake two important tasks: the provision of objective information about the activities of the state and other role players, and the facilitation of the new information policy.

5.14.10. To carry out these two functions, two distinct structures will be necessary. At the same time, the information arms of various ministries, especially those dealing with reconstruction and development, must be strengthened.

5.14.11. All these measures require institutional mechanisms independent of the democratic government and representative of society as a whole. Some of the more crucial ones are:

5.14.11.1. Information Development Trust: made up of civil society, media role players, especially community-based ones, the democratic government and political interests, to work out detailed criteria and mechanisms for assisting relevant media enterprises.

5.14.11.2. Independent Broadcasting Authority (IBA): appointed in a transparent and participatory process. Made up of persons of integrity and experts in the broadcasting field. Responsible for the issuing of broadcasting licences and other broadcasting regulations.

5.14.11.3. Public Broadcaster Board: appointed in a similar manner to give broad direction to the public broadcaster, without undermining editorial independence.

5.14.11.4. Voluntary regulatory mechanisms: for private media enterprise, and representative of all role players, including media workers. Within broadcasting, the voluntary regulations should be within the framework provided by the IBA.

5.14.11.5. Independent unions of media workers and associations of owners of media institutions.

6.
Implementing the RDP

6.1 PROBLEM STATEMENT

6.1.1. The processes of planning and development in South Africa have been structurally distorted by the objectives of apartheid and, both by design and default, have failed to meet the needs of the majority. In recent years all parts of South Africa's excessively complex state system have been incapable of implementing their stated goals. Increased waste, unused funds and outright corruption have characterised government. To implement the RDP, a thoroughgoing reform will be necessary to address the following major structural weaknesses:

6.1.1.1. Excessive departmentalism leading to uncoordinated, sometimes contradictory, decision-making by various state agencies.

6.1.1.2. The allocation of power between the various tiers of government – local, regional and national – does not accord with practical needs. Generally, the central state and some regional governments have excessive and inappropriate power.

6.1.1.3. At all levels, the structures of government exclude the majority of the population from participation in decision-making. Bureaucrats do not consult with most stakeholders.

6.1.1.4. Decision-making remains largely unaccountable either to the public or to monitoring structures. Typically, civil servants act in secret. They rarely justify or explain their decisions in public, and they often have poor relations with NGOs, civics and other community organisations.

6.1.1.5.   The potential contribution of NGOs to reconstruction and development is reduced by the lack of an overall framework and integrative programmes. This results in fragmented and isolated projects.

6.1.1.6.   Implementation of any development programme under circumstances of violence and corruption or clientelism is extremely difficult. The problems worsen in marginalised rural areas where the right-wing or bantustan authorities hold power.

6.2   VISION AND OBJECTIVES

6.2.1.   The basic principles of the RDP are that it is a coherent programme, that it builds a nation, that it is people-driven, that it provides peace and security for all, that it links reconstruction and development, and that it democratises the state and society. This approach has not been attempted in South Africa, and is a fundamental break with apartheid practices. This imposes major new challenges in how to implement such a programme.

6.2.2.   Accordingly, specific structures are necessary to implement the RDP; their functions will be:

6.2.2.1.   to manage policy and the ability to determine spending priorities within a strategic perspective;

6.2.2.2.   to coordinate resources and actions;

6.2.2.3.   to incorporate all major stakeholders in establishing, implementing and evaluating policy;

6.2.2.4.   to establish legislative, procedural, institutional and financial frameworks that ensure that policies can be implemented;

6.2.2.5.   to ensure adequate funding of integrated programmes and that resources reach the targeted communities;

6.2.2.6.   to facilitate the management of potential conflict over limited resources and differing needs, and

6.2.2.7.   to ensure a macro-economic policy environment that is stable.

6.2.3.   Financing the RDP presents both a challenge and an opportunity to revive our economy and set it on a path to sustained reconstruction and development. We must finance the RDP in ways that preserve macro-economic balances, especially in terms of avoiding undue inflation and balance-of-payments difficulties. This requires a strategic approach that combines public and private sector funding, taking into account the sequence and timing of funding sources and programmes.

6.3   IMPLEMENTING AND COORDINATING STRUCTURES

6.3.1.   To implement the RDP will require the establishment of effective RDP structures within national, provincial and local governments. These structures must monitor the implementation of the RDP, including the elaboration of planning frameworks and coordination between departments and tiers of government.

6.3.2.   A prime function of these structures will be to overcome tendencies to fragmentation of different government departments. While not displacing the line functions of other departments, the structures will require real powers of coordination and an appropriate budget. The national RDP structure should also have oversight of inter-governmental financial transfers (national to provincial, provincial to local, etc.) to ensure that these are in conformity with the overall national objectives of the RDP.

6.3.3.   The democratic government must undertake a review of all ministries, parastatals and other democratic government agencies, in conjunction with the Public Service Commission and the Financial and Fiscal Commission, in order to assess their abilities and willingness to achieve the goals and objectives of the RDP.

6.3.4. Democratic government and parastatal programmes must be based on publicly-determined priorities in line with the RDP, and appropriate priority-setting mechanisms must be established. Each institution of government should establish a public priority-setting exercise, whose objectives should be measurable, achievable, have a defined time frame and be accompanied by a plan and budget to accomplish them. A performance audit of government programmes and agencies must be carried out within six months of the inauguration of the Interim Government of National Unity, and regularly thereafter.

6.3.5. The RDP national coordinating body must also ensure that the structures of civil society are involved in the programme. It must ensure coordination between the various ministries, parastatals, labour, civic and other organisations. It must link with existing sectoral and development forums at national level, in order to establish effective systems of coordination. Similar bodies should be established at provincial and local levels. In addition, provincial and local development forums are important vehicles for ensuring the participation of local communities and interest groups in the development process. Development forums must be strengthened through the provision of adequate resources.

6.3.6. The RDP recognises that access to planning procedures and information is unequally weighted in favour of an already privileged group. The RDP structures must ensure that historically oppressed communities get the resources they need to participate meaningfully in planning processes and decision-making. Particular emphasis must be placed on the role of women in urban and rural areas and in micro enterprises.

6.4 PLANNING FRAMEWORKS

6.4.1. The Interim Constitution lays the basis for new relationships between national, provincial and local government. The intention of the RDP is to establish a national framework that guides provincial government and allocates appropriate powers and functions to these levels. This requires considerable interaction and coordination between national, provincial and local structures. The objective is to establish a framework to which statutory authorities should relate, and to guide both public and private investment decisions to ensure the best cumulative results.

6.4.2.   The democratic government will reduce the burden of implementation which falls upon its shoulders through the appropriate allocation of powers and responsibilities to lower levels of government, and through the active involvement of organisations of civil society. By providing a coherent framework it will be able to mobilise considerable energy behind the RDP and ensure that it meets the practical requirements of designing programmes in different areas.

6.4.3.   In order to ensure a coherent and effective implementation of the RDP, a planning process must establish a clear hierarchy of areas of responsibility, roles of sub-national plans, guidelines for decision-making, strategy formulation, and procedures. Planning guidelines must also subordinate local planning to metropolitan/district, provincial and national development planning (for example, by reducing the status of zoning and town-planning schemes to the status of local plans which are automatically overridden by higher levels of planning).

6.4.4.   The RDP must be based on a coordinated and coherent development strategy. This strategy in turn must operate within frameworks at national, provincial and local levels that:

6.4.4.1.   focus on the development challenges and the strategies to meet these challenges (frameworks at provincial and local level must address institutional, social, economic, fiscal, cultural and physical planning requirements appropriate to that level of authority);

6.4.4.2.   provide coherent and coordinated guidelines within which appropriate statutory authorities can function;

6.4.4.3.   guide work programming and priorities, development actions, participatory processes, and priority-based budgeting, and

6.4.4.4.   guide both public and private investment-planning decisions to ensure the best cumulative effects.

6.4.5.   RDP frameworks must be tied to the budgeting process, and revised, updated and tabled in parliament annually. New plan-making processes and approval procedures must be developed. These must be simple and easy to understand and capable of speedy implementation. The RDP requires collaborative, integrated planning and decision-making.

6.4.6.   To ensure the efficacy of the RDP, a national system of monitoring must establish a set of key indicators and measure the impact of the RDP on these indicators. By mid-1994, the central RDP agency must develop criteria for assessing targets and time frames. Every possible step must be taken to ensure that the decision-makers are held accountable for their decisions. They must motivate publicly all decisions with sound reasons. Affected parties must be able to appeal against planning decisions to an independent appeals body.

6.4.7.   **Regulatory system for planning the RDP.**

6.4.7.1.   A new legislative and regulatory system for development planning is required in order to make the RDP a reality. Current inappropriate and unconstitutional development legislation must be repealed.

6.4.7.2.   The regulatory system must provide a basis for defining and fast-tracking strategic reconstruction projects, and provide for rapid granting of legal status to widely supported, interim metropolitan/district and provincial development frameworks.

6.4.7.3. The system should be consolidated in the form of a National Reconstruction and Development Act, and promulgated as a matter of urgency. Simultaneously a prototypical Provincial Reconstruction and Development Planning Act should be developed for consideration and adoption by each province.

6.5 FINANCING THE RDP

6.5.1. The RDP will mean nothing if it cannot be financed. Two questions arise: can we afford such an extensive programme, and will people be required to pay more? If the democratic government were to attempt to finance all the proposals contained in the RDP then the answer to the first question would be a clear 'no' and to the second a clear 'yes' – in other words, the RDP would fail. We must remind ourselves of the six basic principles underlying the RDP as set out in Chapter One. These six principles distinguish the RDP from all other programmes proposed by political parties.

6.5.2. The success of the RDP does not only require finance. It also requires labour, skills and coordinated effort in combination with that finance. The six principles allow for this combination by harnessing the underutilised resources of the democratic government, the private sector, labour communities and women, and by utilising these resources in a rational and effective way. Only the ANC and its allies are capable of such a programme. Finance for the RDP will come from revenues, issuing debt (including general obligation and revenue bonds) and grants. The largest portion of all RDP proposals will be financed by better use of existing resources.

6.5.3. However, it is clear that government policy and mechanisms of raising finance are crucial to the success of the RDP. If they were to cause excessive inflation or serious balance of payments problems they would worsen the position of the poor, curtail growth and cause the RDP to fail. Government contributions to the financing of the RDP must, therefore, avoid undue inflation and balance of payments difficulties. In the long run, the RDP will redirect government spending, rather than increasing it as a proportion of GDP.

6.5.4. The financing of the programme is a national responsibility, and provincial and local governments would not be expected to rely on their own tax bases and resources in its implementation, although contributions from these sources should be made in order to enhance accountability. Allocations from national resources will take into account the existing inequalities between provinces and localities, and will be based on population size, development backlogs, and other objective criteria as may be determined by the Financial and Fiscal Commission.

6.5.5. **Restructuring the national budget**. Despite relatively high levels of government spending, South Africa displays a worse record than many poorer countries in meeting basic needs. This situation reflects the impact of apartheid in terms of both racially skewed spending and corrupt, unaccountable government. In addition, low growth rates and an absence of growth-promoting capital expenditure by the public sector created fiscal problems. A severe imbalance exists at present between insufficient capital expenditure and excessive consumption expenditure.

6.5.6. The RDP is, therefore, committed to a programme of restructuring public expenditure to finance the democratic government's contribution to the RDP. Given the fiscal malaise left by apartheid, careful programmes must be developed around financing increased capital expenditure, increasing the efficiency of consumption expenditure and improving the revenue-recovery capacities of the government.

6.5.7. The existing ratios of the deficit, borrowing and taxation to GNP are part of our macro-economic problem. In meeting the financing needs of the RDP and retaining macro stability during its implementation, particular attention will be paid to these ratios. The emphasis will be on ensuring a growing GDP, improved revenue recovery, and more effective expenditure in order to make more resources available. In the process of raising new funds and applying them, the ratios mentioned above must be taken into account.

6.5.8.   The democratic government must end unnecessary secrecy in the formulation of the budget. To that end, it must change the relevant regulations. We must establish a Parliamentary Budget Office with sufficient resources and personnel to ensure efficient democratic oversight of the budget. Transformation of the parastatals and cooperation with forums will also help ensure more efficient and open budgeting processes.

6.5.9.   Efficient and open transformation of the budget requires the development of a five-year fiscal plan as the framework for multi-year budgets.

6.5.10. By combining the ministries of State Expenditure and Finance to form a single finance ministry, we will reduce duplication and streamline decision-making.

6.5.11. The democratic government must make the development of effective and open performance auditing a top priority. Auditing of public institutions must broaden from its narrow focus on financial accountability to assess how well expenditures meet RDP targets. The Interim Constitution gives the Auditor-General responsibility for performance auditing mandated by the President. We must begin to define the priority sectors and agencies for performance auditing.

6.5.12. The democratic government must mandate the Financial and Fiscal Commission to review the tax structure in order to develop a more progressive, fair and transparent structure. Priorities will include:

6.5.12.1. eliminating bias in tax against women regardless of marital status, and recognising women's child-care costs and the unpaid labour they perform;

6.5.12.2. reviewing personal income tax to reduce the burden caused by fiscal drag on middle-income people;

6.5.12.3. rationalising company tax breaks for health, education, housing and other expenditures which may conflict with RDP priorities;

6.5.12.4. simplifying the unnecessarily complex company tax system, which is biased against small and medium-sized enterprises and leads to low effective tax rates despite a fairly high nominal rate, and

6.5.12.5. zero-rating VAT on basic necessities.

6.5.13. Taxation policies should provide incentives for institutional affirmative action programmes covering race and gender, with respect to employment and education.

6.5.14. All macro-economic allocations must be accompanied by social and economic impact analyses on gender, race, urban-rural dimensions, class/income distribution, regional inequalities, and age (to encompass marginalised young people and pensioners). Future budgetary allocations must concretely show the commitment of a future government to women's development and empowerment. The budget should be gender-sensitive. It should contain a social impact statement detailing how budgetary allocations affect women with respect to workload, income, education and career options.

6.5.15. **Mobilising new funds.** The democratic government should establish a Reconstruction Fund (possibly incorporating the wholesale financing requirements of the Electrification Fund and Housing Bank) for elements of the RDP that can generate income streams in the future. The Reconstruction Fund should include some form of dedicated reconstruction bond. In addition, it should draw on specific reconstruction levies. The design of reconstruction levies will depend on the aims of the RDP as a whole, especially in terms of promoting development and growth, but could include levies on capital transfers, land and luxury goods.

6.5.16. There is a need for an overall foreign debt strategy. The RDP must use foreign debt financing only for those elements of the programme that can potentially increase our capacity for earning foreign exchange. Relationships with international financial institutions such as the World Bank and International Monetary Fund must be conducted in such a way as to protect the integrity of domestic policy formulation and promote the interests of the South African population and the economy. Above all, we must pursue policies that enhance national self-sufficiency and enable us to reduce dependence on international financial institutions. Further, we must introduce measures to ensure that foreign governmental and non-governmental aid supports the RDP.

6.5.17. **Socially desirable investments.** The democratic government cannot fund the RDP without support from the private sector. Financial institutions must assist both by funding individual programmes to meet basic needs, especially housing, and by improving their services to small-scale producers and the black communities. The democratic government must modify regulations and support innovative financial institutions and instruments that will fund the RDP. It must attempt to mobilise a significant proportion of contractual savings, within an appropriate regulatory and financial framework, for socially desirable investments, without affecting the risk profile or decreasing the returns on investment. If the major financial institutions do not take up socially desirable and economically targeted investments, the democratic government should consider some form of legislative compulsion such as prescribed assets.

6.5.18. **Other resources.** The democratic government must not be alone in accessing resources. Unemployed local labour must be mobilised, through job banks and community-based employment-generation initiatives. Employed workers must be given incentives to use their skills and knowledge in the interests of society. Creative use of local resources – such as building materials – must be encouraged. The power of women in households, in production and in community structures must be fully acknowledged and rewarded. Only through such grassroots-oriented development initiatives can the RDP be brought to its logical fruition as a successful programme for all South Africans.

7.
Conclusion

7.1   Throughout this document, we have stressed that the RDP is a people-driven programme. People have been part of drawing up the RDP and they must now take the process forward. How can this be done in concrete ways? A number of processes must now begin.

7.2   The RDP will now be used to consult widely, in order to get comment and further input. Any organisation that wishes to make such a contribution can do so in writing, or contact the ANC to arrange a meeting. Any organisation that feels that it can make a specific contribution to the implementation of the RDP should do likewise.

7.3   We welcome written comment from any organisation, expert or person with knowledge about any of the areas covered in the RDP. Clearly we will not be able to use every comment, and the comments will need to be written within the spirit of the basic principles outlined in Chapter One, the 'Introduction to the RDP'.

7.4   In the provinces and at local levels, the Alliance, the South African National Civics Organisation (SANCO) and the National Education Coordinating Committee (NECC) have begun to apply the RDP framework in their own areas. They are discussing the particular problems their provinces may have, and how their own RDP should address these.

7.5   Material is being produced that will popularise the RDP and allow for its discussion throughout the length and breadth of our land. However, this must not be a process of telling people what the new government's RDP will do for them, but of encouraging people to play an active role in implementing their own RDP with government assistance.

7.6   The Alliance will now be reaching out to many organisations to discuss and receive inputs on the RDP. This support and information will be used as we continue to develop detailed policy. Work groups are being established to develop both policy and programmes of government at national and provincial levels.

7.7   The future is in our hands and we must carry forward the work needed to finally liberate ourselves from the evils of apartheid.

To make an input into the RDP, contact:

The RDP
ANC
P.O. Box 61884
Marshalltown
2107

Telephone: (011) 330-7000